CBSE Term II
2022

Informatics Practices
Class XII

CBSE Term II 2022

Informatics Practices

Class XII

- Complete Theory Covering NCERT
- Case Based Questions
- Short/Long Answer Questions
- 3 Practice Papers with Explanations

Author
Debapriya Chakraborty

ARIHANT PRAKASHAN (School Division Series)

ARIHANT PRAKASHAN (School Division Series)

卐 **Administrative & Production Offices**

Regd. Office

'Ramchhaya' 4577/15, Agarwal Road, Darya Ganj, New Delhi -110002
Tele: 011- 47630600, 43518550

卐 **Head Office**

Kalindi, TP Nagar, Meerut (UP) - 250002, Tel: 0121-7156203, 7156204

卐 **Sales & Support Offices**

Agra, Ahmedabad, Bengaluru, Bareilly, Chennai, Delhi, Guwahati, Hyderabad, Jaipur, Jhansi, Kolkata, Lucknow, Nagpur & Pune.

卐 **ISBN :** 978-93-25797-06-2

卐

PO No : TXT-XX-XXXXXXX-X-XX

Published by Arihant Publications (India) Ltd.

For further information about the books published by Arihant, log on to www.arihantbooks.com or e-mail at info@arihantbooks.com

Follow us on   

Contents

Syllabus
CBSE Term II Class XII

Distribution of Theory Marks

No.	Units	Marks
2.	Database Query using SQL	25
3.	Introduction to Computer Networks	10
	Total	**35**

Unit 2 Database Query using SQL

- Math functions: POWER (), ROUND (), MOD ().
- Text functions: UCASE ()/UPPER (), LCASE ()/LOWER (), MID ()/SUBSTRING ()/SUBSTR (), LENGTH (), LEFT (), RIGHT (), INSTR (), LTRIM (), RTRIM (), TRIM ().
- Date Functions: NOW (), DATE (), MONTH (), MONTHNAME (), YEAR (), DAY (), DAYNAME (). Aggregate Functions: MAX (), MIN (), AVG (), SUM (), COUNT (); using COUNT (*).
- Querying and manipulating data using Group by, Having, Order by.

Unit 3 Introduction to Computer Networks

- Introduction to networks, Types of network: LAN, MAN, WAN.
- Network Devices: modem, hub, switch, repeater, router, gateway.
- Network Topologies: Star, Bus, Tree, Mesh.
- Introduction to Internet, URL, WWW and its applications- Web, email, Chat, VoIP.
- Website: Introduction, difference between a website and webpage, static vs dynamic web page, web server and hosting of a website.
- Web Browsers: Introduction, commonly used browsers, browser settings, add-ons and plug-ins, cookies.

CBSE Circular

Exam Scheme Term I & II

केन्द्रीय माध्यमिक शिक्षा बोर्ड

(शिक्षा मंत्रालय, भारत सरकार के अधीन एक स्वायत संगठन)

CENTRAL BOARD OF SECONDARY EDUCATION

(An Autonomous Organisation under the Ministryof Education, Govt. of India)

CBSE/DIR (ACAD)/2021

Date: July 05, 2021
Circular No: Acad-51/2021

All the Heads of Schools affiliated to CBSE

Subject: Special Scheme of Assessment for Board Examination Classes X and XII for the Session 2021-22

COVID 19 pandemic caused almost all CBSE schools to function in a virtual mode for most part of the academic session of 2020-21. Due to the extreme risk associated with the conduct of Board examinations during the second wave in April 2021, CBSE had to cancel both its class X and XII Board examinations of the year 2021 and results are to be declared on the basis of a credible, reliable, flexible and valid alternative assessment policy. This, in turn, also necessitated deliberations over alternative ways to look at the learning objectives as well as the conduct of the Board Examinations for the academic session 2021-22 in case the situation remains unfeasible.

CBSE has also held stake holder consultations with Government schools as well as private independent schools from across the country especially schools from the remote rural areas and a majority of them have requested for the rationalization of the syllabus, similar to last year in view of reduced time permitted for organizing online classes. The Board has also considered the concerns regarding differential availability of electronic gadgets, connectivity and effectiveness of online teaching and other socio-economic issues specially with respect to students from economically weaker section and those residing in far flung areas of the country. In a survey conducted by CBSE, it was revealed that the rationalized syllabus notified for the session 2020-21 was effective for schools in covering the syllabus and helped learners in achieving learning objectives in a less stressful manner.

In the above backdrop and in line with the Board's continued focus on assessing stipulated learning outcomes by making the examinations competencies and core concepts based, student-centric, transparent, technology-driven, and having advance provision of alternatives for different future scenarios, the following schemes are introduced for the Academic Session for Class X and Class XII 2021-22.

केन्द्रीय माध्यमिक शिक्षा बोर्ड

(शिक्षा मंत्रालय, भारत सरकार के अधीन एक स्वायत संगठन)

CENTRAL BOARD OF SECONDARY EDUCATION

(An Autonomous Organisation under the Ministryof Education, Govt. of India)

Special Scheme for 2021-22

A. Academic session to be divided into 2 Terms with approximately 50% syllabus in each term:

The syllabus for the Academic session 2021-22 will be divided into 2 terms by following a systematic approach by looking into the interconnectivity of concepts and topics by the Subject Experts and the Board will conduct examinations at the end of each term on the basis of the bifurcated syllabus. This is done to increase the probability of having a Board conducted classes X and XII examinations at the end of the academic session.

B. The syllabus for the Board examination 2021-22 will be rationalized similar to that of the last academic session to be notified in July 2021. For academic transactions, however, schools will follow the curriculum and syllabus released by the Board vide Circular no. F.1001/CBSE-Acad/Curriculum/2021 dated 31 March 2021, Schools will also use alternative academic calendar and inputs from the NCERT on transacting the curriculum.

C. Efforts will be made to make Internal Assessment/ Practical/ Project work more credible and valid as per the guidelines and Moderation Policy to be announced by the Board to ensure fair distribution of marks.

Details of Curriculum Transaction

- Schools will continue teaching in distance mode till the authorities permit in-person mode of teaching in schools.

- **Classes IX-X: Internal Assessment** (throughout the year-irrespective of Term I and II) would include the *3 periodic tests, student enrichment, portfolio and practical work/ speaking listening activities/ project.*

- **Classes XI-XII: Internal Assessment** (throughout the year-irrespective of Term I and II) would include end of topic or unit tests/ exploratory activities/ practicals/ projects.

- Schools would create a student profile for all assessment undertaken over the year and retain the evidences in digital format.

- CBSE will facilitate schools to upload marks of Internal Assessment on the CBSE IT platform.

- Guidelines for Internal Assessment for all subjects will also be released along with the rationalized term wise divided syllabus for the session 2021-22.The Board would also provide additional resources like sample assessments, question banks, teacher training etc. for more reliable and valid internal assessments.

केन्द्रीय माध्यमिक शिक्षा बोर्ड

(शिक्षा मंत्रालय, भारत सरकार के अधीन एक स्वायत संगठन)

CENTRAL BOARD OF SECONDARY EDUCATION

(An Autonomous Organisation under the Ministryof Education, Govt. of India)

Term I Examinations:

- At the end of the first term, the Board will organize **Term I Examination** in a flexible schedule to be conducted between November-December 2021 with a window period of 4-8 weeks for schools situated in different parts of country and abroad. Dates for conduct of examinations will be notified subsequently.

- The Question Paper will have Multiple Choice Questions (MCQ) including case-based MCQs and MCQs on assertion-reasoning type. Duration of test will be **90 minutes** and it will cover only the rationalized syllabus of **Term I only** (i.e. approx. 50% of the entire syllabus).

- Question Papers will be sent by the CBSE to schools along with marking scheme.

- The exams will be conducted under the supervision of the External Center Superintendents and Observers appointed by CBSE.

- The responses of students will be captured on OMR sheets which, after scanning may be directly uploaded at CBSE portal or alternatively may be evaluated and marks obtained will be uploaded by the school on the very same day. The final direction in this regard will be conveyed to schools by the Examination Unit of the Board.

- Marks of the **Term I** Examination will contribute to the final overall score of students.

Term II Examination/ Year-end Examination:

- At the end of the second term, the Board would organize **Term II or Year-end Examination** based on the rationalized syllabus of Term II only (i.e. approximately 50% of the entire syllabus).

- This examination would be held around **March-April 2022** at the examination centres fixed by the Board.

- The paper will be of **2 hours duration** and have questions of different formats (case-based/ situation based, open ended- short answer/ long answer type).

- In case the situation is not conducive for normal descriptive examination a **90 minute MCQ based exam** will be conducted at the end of the Term II also.

- Marks of the Term II Examination would contribute to the final overall score.

केन्द्रीय माध्यमिक शिक्षा बोर्ड

(शिक्षा मंत्रालय, भारत सरकार के अधीन एक स्वायत संगठन)

CENTRAL BOARD OF SECONDARY EDUCATION

(An Autonomous Organisation under the Ministryof Education, Govt. of India)

<u>Assessment / Examination as per different situations</u>

A. In case the situation of the pandemic improves and students are able to come to schools or centres for taking the exams.

Board would conduct Term I and Term II examinations at schools/centres and the theory marks will be distributed equally between the two exams.

B. In case the situation of the pandemic forces complete closure of schools during November-December 2021, but Term II exams are held at schools or centres.

Term I MCQ based examination would be done by students online/offline from home - in this case, the weightage of this exam for the final score would be reduced, and weightage of Term II exams will be increased for declaration of final result

C. In case the situation of the pandemic forces complete closure of schools during March-April 2022, but Term I exams are held at schools or centres.

Results would be based on the performance of students on Term I MCQ based examination and internal assessments. The weightage of marks of Term I examination conducted by the Board will be increased to provide year end results of candidates.

D. In case the situation of the pandemic forces complete closure of schools and Board conducted Term I and II exams are taken by the candidates from home in the session 2021-22.

Results would be computed on the basis of the Internal Assessment/Practical/Project Work and Theory marks of Term-I and II exams taken by the candidate from home in Class X / XII subject to the moderation or other measures to ensure validity and reliability of the assessment.

In all the above cases, data analysis of marks of students will be undertaken to ensure the integrity of internal assessments and home based exams.

Dr. Joseph Emmanuel
Director (Academics)

CHAPTER 01

MySQL Functions and Querying using SQL

In this Chapter...

- Types of SQL Functions
- Mathematical Functions
- String/Text Functions
- Date/Time Functions

MySQL function performs a pre-defined task and returns a single value such as a numerical, string or date/time value. Functions operate on zero, one, two or more values provided to them, these values are called parameters or arguments. MySQL support number of built-in functions.

To use any function, we need to specify the column to which the function should be applied.

```
e.g. SELECT function(column_name)
     FROM table_name;
```

To specify multiple columns, you can write as follows:

```
e.g. SELECT *, function(column_name)
     FROM table_name;
or   SELECT column_name1,function(column_name2),
                               column_name3
     FROM table_name;
```

Types of SQL Functions

SQL provides two types of functions, which are as follows :

(i) **Single-row Functions** This type of function work with a single-row at a time.

It returns a result for each row of the table, on which the query is performed. Examples of single-row functions include CHAR(),CONCAT(), INSTR(), etc.

(ii) **Multiple-row Functions** This type of function work with data of multiple-rows at a time and return a single output value.

Examples of multiple-row functions include SUM(), AVG(), COUNT(), etc.

Mathematical Functions

MySQL provides a number of functions used for performing mathematical calculations on database. Mathematical functions are very important in SQL to implement different mathematical concepts in queries. Some mathematical functions are explained with examples as follows:

POWER()/POW()

This function returns the value of a number raised to the power of another number.

Syntax POWER(M,N) or POW(M,N)

where, M is the base and N is an exponent.

```
e.g. mysql> SELECT POWER(2,2);
```

The above query produces the following output:

```
+----------+
| POWER(2,2)|
+----------+
|        4 |
+----------+
```

```
mysql> SELECT POWER(2,-3);
```

The above query produces the following output:

```
+----------+
| POWER(2,-3)|
+----------+
|    0.125 |
+----------+
```

```
mysql> SELECT POWER(30,0.2);
```

The above query produces the following output :

```
+------------------+
| POWER(30,0.2)    |
+------------------+
| 1.97435048583482 |
+------------------+
```

ROUND()

This function rounds up the number to the upwards or downwards to the nearest whole number.

Syntax `ROUND(M,N)` or `ROUND(M)`

where, M is the number to be rounded off and N is the number of places to which the number should be rounded off. If N is not specified, then it is assumed zero (0).

e.g. `mysql> SELECT ROUND(4.65,1);`

The above query produces the following output:

```
+-------------+
| ROUND(4.65,1) |
+-------------+
|         4.7 |
+-------------+
```

`mysql> SELECT ROUND (-5.43);`

The above query produces the following output:

```
+-------------+
| ROUND(-5.43) |
+-------------+
|          -5 |
+-------------+
```

`mysql> SELECT ROUND (5.43);`

The above query produces the following output:

```
+-------------+
| ROUND(5.43) |
+-------------+
|           5 |
+-------------+
```

`mysql> SELECT ROUND (1.645,0);`

The above query produces the following output:

```
+-------------+
| ROUND(1.645,0) |
+-------------+
|           2 |
+-------------+
```

`mysql> SELECT ROUND (3.45,-1);`

The above query produces the following output:

```
+-------------+
| ROUND(3.45, -1) |
+-------------+
|           0 |
+-------------+
```

MOD()

This function returns the remainder of a number dividing by another number.

Syntax `MOD(Dividend, Divisor)`

e.g. `mysql> SELECT MOD(11,4);`

The above query produces the following output:

```
+----------+
| MOD(11,4) |
+----------+
|        3 |
+----------+
```

`mysql> SELECT MOD(-25,7);`

The above query produces the following output:

```
+----------+
| MOD(-25,7) |
+----------+
|        -4 |
+----------+
```

`mysql> SELECT MOD(25.4,7);`

The above query produces the following output:

```
+-----------+
| MOD(25.4,7) |
+-----------+
|        4.4 |
+-----------+
```

String/Text Functions

The string/text functions of SQL are used to extract, change, format or alter character strings. They accept a character string as an input and provides character string or numeric values as an output. Some string/text functions are explained with example as follows :

UPPER()/UCASE()

This function converts the characters of a string into the uppercase characters.

Syntax `UPPER(str/column_name)`

or   `UCASE(str/column_name)`

e.g. `mysql> SELECT UPPER('mystring');`

The above query produces the following output:

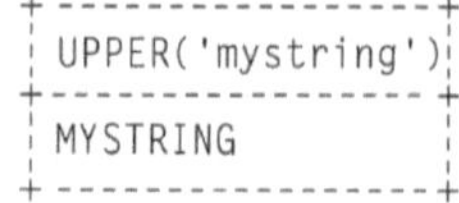

```
+------------------+
| UPPER('mystring') |
+------------------+
| MYSTRING         |
+------------------+
```

Table : Item

Icode	Descp	Price	QOH	Sold
101	Stationary	54.89	700	350
102	Food	650.78	1200	340
103	Sports	700.90	3000	500
104	Food	1400.00	900	120
105	Sports	6700.00	790	540

e.g. Write a query to display the item description in uppercase letter from table Item.

`mysql> SELECT UPPER(Descp) FROM Item;`

The above query produces the following output:

```
+-------------+
| UPPER(Descp) |
+-------------+
| STATIONARY  |
| FOOD        |
| SPORTS      |
| FOOD        |
| SPORTS      |
+-------------+
```

or `mysql> SELECT UCASE(Descp) FROM Item;`

The above query produces the following output:

```
+-----------------+
| UCASE(Descp)    |
+-----------------+
| STATIONARY      |
| FOOD            |
| SPORTS          |
| FOOD            |
| SPORTS          |
+-----------------+
```

LOWER()/LCASE()

This function converts the characters of an argument string to the lowercase characters. The return value has the same data type as the argument.

Syntax LOWER(str/column_name)

or   LCASE(str/column_name)

e.g. mysql> SELECT LOWER('MYSQL');

The above query produces the following output:

```
+---------------+
| LOWER('MYSQL')|
+---------------+
| mysql         |
+---------------+
```

e.g. Write a query to display the item description in lowercase letter from table Item.

    mysql> SELECT LOWER(Descp) FROM Item;

The above query produces the following output:

```
+-------------+
| LOWER(Descp)|
+-------------+
| stationary  |
| food        |
| sports      |
| food        |
| sports      |
+-------------+
```

or   mysql> SELECT LCASE(Descp) FROM Item;

The above query produces the following output:

```
+-------------+
| LCASE(Descp)|
+-------------+
| stationary  |
| food        |
| sports      |
| food        |
| sports      |
+-------------+
```

SUBSTRING()/SUBSTR()/MID()

This function returns the substring specified number of characters) from a particular position of a given string.

Syntax SUBSTR(str/column_name,pos,len)

or   SUBSTRING(str/column_name,pos,len)

or   MID(str/column_name,pos,len)

where, str is a string from which a substring is returned, pos is an integer indicating the string position and len is an integer indicating the length of the substring.

e.g. mysql> SELECT SUBSTR
                  ('EASYCALCULATION',5,11);

The above query produces the following output:

```
+----------------------------------+
| SUBSTR('EASYCALCULATION',5,11)   |
+----------------------------------+
| CALCULATION                      |
+----------------------------------+
```

mysql> SELECT SUBSTR
                  ('EASYCALCULATION',7);

The above query produces the following output:

```
+------------------------------+
| SUBSTR('EASYCALCULATION',7)  |
+------------------------------+
| LCULATION                    |
+------------------------------+
```

Write the output of the following command.

    mysql> SELECT SUBSTR(Descp,3,4) FROM Item
    WHERE QOH=700;

The above query produces the following output:

```
+------------------+
| SUBSTR(Descp,3,4)|
+------------------+
| atio             |
+------------------+
```

Write the output of the following command.

    mysql> SELECT MID('Informatics
    Practices',2,8);

The above query will produce the following output:

```
+----------------------------------+
| MID('Informatics Practices',2,8) |
+----------------------------------+
| nformati                         |
+----------------------------------+
```

Write the output of the following command.

    mysql> SELECT UPPER(MID(Descp,2,8)) FROM
    Item WHERE Icode=101;

The above query will produce the following output:

```
+---------------------+
| UPPER(MID(Descp,2,8))|
+---------------------+
| TATIONAR            |
+---------------------+
```

LENGTH()

This function returns the length of the string in bytes. It includes the count of blank spaces in the string.

Syntax LENGTH(string/column_name)

e.g. mysql> SELECT LENGTH('easycalculation');

Above query produces the following output :

```
+---------------------------+
| LENGTH('easycalculation') |
+---------------------------+
| 15                        |
+---------------------------+
```

Write a query to display the item code and length of each item's description.

```
mysql> SELECT Icode, LENGTH(Descp) FROM
Item;
```

Above query produces the following output:

```
+-------+---------------+
! Icode | LENGTH(Descp) !
+-------+---------------+
! 101   !            10 !
! 102   !             4 !
! 103   !             6 !
! 104   !             4 !
! 105   !             6 !
+-------+---------------+
```

LEFT()

This function returns a specified number of characters from the left of the string. This function returns NULL, if any argument is NULL.

Syntax `LEFT(string,length)`

e.g. `mysql> SELECT LEFT('India',3);`

Above query produces the following output:

```
+--------------+
!LEFT('India',3)!
+--------------+
! Ind          !
+--------------+
```

Table: Empdetail

EmpNo	EmpName	EmpAdd	EmpSal
E01	Ajay	Jaipur	45000.00
E02	Vimal	Chennai	60000.00
E03	Vinay	Jabalpur	56000.00
E04	Rina	Delhi	90000.00

e.g. Write a query to view first three characters of employee's name from the table Empdetail.

```
mysql> SELECT LEFT(EmpName,3) FROM
Empdetail;
```

Above query produces the following output:

```
+----------------+
! LEFT(EmpName,3) !
+----------------+
! Aja            !
! Vim            !
! Vin            !
! Rin            !
+----------------+
```

RIGHT()

Working of this function is just reverse of LEFT function. It returns a specified number of characters from the right of the string. This function returns NULL, if any argument is NULL.

Syntax `RIGHT(string,length)`

e.g. `mysql> SELECT RIGHT('India',3);`

Above query produces the following output:

```
+----------------+
! RIGHT('India',3)!
+----------------+
! dia            !
+----------------+
```

e.g. Write a query to view last three characters of employee's address from the table Empdetail.

```
mysql> SELECT RIGHT(EmpAdd,3) FROM
Empdetail;
```

Above query produces the following output:

```
+----------------+
! RIGHT(EmpAdd,3) !
+----------------+
! pur            !
! nai            !
! pur            !
! lhi            !
+----------------+
```

INSTR()

This function takes a string and a substring of it as arguments and returns an integer which indicates the position of the first occurrence of the substring within the string.

Syntax `INSTR(ori_str/column_name, sub_str)`

where, ori_str is the string to be searched and sub_str is the string to be searched from ori_str.

e.g. `mysql> SELECT INSTR('firstexam','e');`

Above query produces the following output:

```
+----------------------+
! INSTR('firstexam','e')!
+----------------------+
!                    6 !
+----------------------+
```

e.g. Consider all the names of employees from Empdetail table. Write a query to find the position of letter 'i' in Empdetail table, where employee salary is between 50000 and 60000.

```
mysql> SELECT EmpName, INSTR(EmpName,'i')
FROM Empdetail
WHERE EmpSal BETWEEN 50000 AND 60000;
```

Above query produces the following output:

```
+---------+--------------------+
! EmpName ! INSTR(EmpName,'i') !
+---------+--------------------+
! Vimal   !                  2 !
! Vinay   !                  2 !
+---------+--------------------+
```

TRIM()

This function is used to return a string after removing all prefix or suffix spaces from the given string.

Syntax `TRIM([{BOTH|LEADING|TRAILING} [remstr] FROM] str/column_name)`

Here, **BOTH** indicates the prefixes and suffixes from both left and right are to be removed.

LEADING indicates only the leading prefixes are to be removed.

TRAILING indicates only the trailing suffixes are to be removed.

remstr is the string to be removed. It is optional, if not specified and spaces are removed.

FROM it is a keyword.

str is a string from where remstr is to be removed.

e.g. **Case 1** If no specifier is given, BOTH is assumed and the string is trimmed from both end.

```
mysql> SELECT TRIM(' India ');
```

Above query produces the following output:

```
+-----------------+
| TRIM(' India ') |
+-----------------+
| India           |
+-----------------+
```

Case 2 If leading specifier is given, then the prefix part is trimmed.

```
mysql> SELECT TRIM(LEADING '!'
FROM '!!!!India!!!!');
```

Above query produces the following output:

```
+-------------------------------------+
| TRIM(LEADING '!' FROM '!!!!India!!!!') |
+-------------------------------------+
| India!!!!                           |
+-------------------------------------+
```

Case 3 If trailing specifier is given, then the suffix part is trimmed.

```
mysql> SELECT TRIM (TRAILING '!' FROM
'!!!!India!!!!');
```

Above query produces the following output:

```
+----------------------------------------+
| TRIM(TRAILING'!'FROM'!!!!India!!!!')   |
+----------------------------------------+
| !!!!India                              |
+----------------------------------------+
```

LTRIM()

This function removes the leading spaces from the characters of a string passed as an argument. Spaces in the middle or trailing spaces are not removed.

Syntax LTRIM(str/column_name)

e.g. mysql> SELECT LTRIM('It is a string argument');

Above query produces the following output:

```
+---------------------------------------+
| LTRIM ('  It is a string argument')   |
+---------------------------------------+
| It is a string argument               |
+---------------------------------------+
```

RTRIM()

This function removes the trailing space from the characters of a string passed as an argument. Spaces in the middle or leading spaces are not removed.

Syntax RTRIM(str/column_name)

e.g. mysql> SELECT RTRIM('It is a string argument');

Above query produces the following output:

```
+-----------------------------------------+
| RTRIM ('It is a string argument    ')   |
+-----------------------------------------+
| It is a string argument                 |
+-----------------------------------------+
```

Date/Time Functions

MySQL stores date in date/time format, representing the century, month, year, day and hours. The date and time functions are used to perform operations on the date/time data stored in the database. The default date format is YYYY-MM-DD in MySQL.

Some date/time functions are explained with examples as follows:

DATE()

This function returns only DATE part from the given date/time argument.

Syntax Date(dt)

Here, dt is the DateTime expression.

e.g. mysql> SELECT DATE('2021-09-30 20:29:13');

Above query produces the following output:

```
+---------------------------+
| DATE('2021-09-30 20:29:13') |
+---------------------------+
| 2021-09-30                |
+---------------------------+
```

MONTH()

This function returns the MONTH part from the date argument within a range of 1 to 12 (January to December) and it returns 0 if MONTH part of the date contains NULL.

Syntax MONTH(date/column_name)

e.g. mysql> SELECT MONTH('2021-09-30');

Above query produces the following output:

```
+---------------------+
| MONTH('2021-09-30') |
+---------------------+
|          9          |
+---------------------+
```

Table: Club

Coach_id	Coachname	Age	Sports	Dateofapp	Pay	Sex
1	KUKRAJA	35	KARATE	1996-03-27	1000.00	M
2	RAVINA	34	KARATE	1998-01-20	1200.00	F
3	KARAN	34	SQUASH	1998-02-19	2000.00	M

Write a query to display the month of all applicants whose age is 35.

```
mysql> SELECT MONTH(Dateofapp) FROM Club
WHERE Age=35;
```

Above query produces the following output:

```
+-----------------+
| MONTH(Dateofapp) |
+-----------------+
|        3         |
+-----------------+
```

MONTHNAME()

This function returns the name of the month from a date specified as an argument.

Syntax `MONTHNAME(date/column_name)`

e.g. `mysql> SELECT MONTHNAME('2021-09-30');`

Above query produces the following output:

```
+-----------------------+
| MONTHNAME('2021-09-30') |
+-----------------------+
| September             |
+-----------------------+
```

Write a query to display the month of application for all coaches whose getting more than 1200 as pay.

```
mysql> SELECT MONTHNAME(Dateofapp) FROM
Club WHERE Pay>=1200;
```

Above query produces the following output:

```
+---------------------+
| MONTHNAME(Dateofapp) |
+---------------------+
| January             |
| February            |
+---------------------+
```

DAY()

This function returns the day of the month (from 1 to 31) from a date specified as an argument.

Syntax `DAY(date/column_name)`

e.g. `mysql> SELECT DAY('2021-09-30');`

Above query produces the following output:

```
+------------------+
| DAY('2021-09-30') |
+------------------+
|               30 |
+------------------+
```

Write a query to display the day of application for all coaches whose getting more than 1200 as pay.

```
mysql> SELECT DAY(Dateofapp) FROM Club
WHERE Pay>=1200;
```

Above query produces the following output:

```
+----------------+
| DAY(Dateofapp) |
+----------------+
|             20 |
|             19 |
+----------------+
```

YEAR()

This function returns the YEAR part from the given date argument. The return value is in the range of 1000 to 9999 or 0 for null date.

Syntax `YEAR(date/column_name)`

e.g. `mysql> SELECT YEAR('2021-09-30');`

Above query produces the following output:

```
+-------------------+
| YEAR('2021-09-30') |
+-------------------+
|              2021 |
+-------------------+
```

Write a query to display the year of application for all female coaches.

```
mysql> SELECT YEAR(Dateofapp) FROM Club
WHERE Sex='F';
```

Above query produces the following output:

```
+-----------------+
| YEAR(Dateofapp) |
+-----------------+
|            1998 |
+-----------------+
```

DAYNAME()

It returns the name of the week day from a date specified as an argument.

Syntax `DAYNAME(date/column_name)`

e.g. `mysql> SELECT DAYNAME ('2021-09-30');`

Above query produces the following output:

```
+----------------------+
| DAYNAME('2021-09-30') |
+----------------------+
| Thursday             |
+----------------------+
```

Write a query to display the day name of application for all female coaches.

```
mysql> SELECT DAYNAME(Dateofapp) FROM
Club WHERE Sex='F';
```

Above query produces the following output:

```
+-------------------+
| DAYNAME(Dateofapp) |
+-------------------+
| Tuesday           |
+-------------------+
```

NOW()

This function returns the current date and time in the format 'YYYY-MM-DD HH:MM:SS' or YYYYMMDDHHMMSS format.

Syntax `NOW()`

e.g. `mysql> SELECT NOW();`

Above query produces the following output:

```
+---------------------+
| NOW()               |
+---------------------+
| 2021-09-30 21:22:07 |
+---------------------+
```

Chapter Practice

Objective Questions

• Multiple Choice Questions

1. Which type of SQL function work with a single-row at a time?
   (a) Multiple-row functions
   (b) Single-row functions
   (c) Both (a) and (b)
   (d) None of the above

Ans. (b) **Single-row functions** work with a single-row at a time. It returns a result for each row of the table, on which the query is performed.

2. Which function accepts a character string as an input and provides character string or numeric values as an output?
   (a) Text   (b) Date
   (c) Time   (d) Math

Ans. (a) Text function accepts a character string as an input and provides character string or numeric values as an output.

3. Which of the following is the correct syntax of LCASE( ) function?
   (a) `LCASE(row_name)`
   (b) `LCE(column_name)`
   (c) `LCASE(str/column_name)`
   (d) None of the above

Ans. (c) This function converts the characters of an argument string to the lowercase characters. The syntax is
`LCASE(str/column_name)` or
`LOWER(str/column_name)`.

4. Which of the following function converts the characters of an argument string to the uppercase characters?
   (a) UCASE( )
   (b) UPPER( )
   (c) Both (a) and (b)
   (d) None of the above

Ans. (c) This function converts the characters of a string into the uppercase characters. The syntax is
`UPPER(str/column_name)` or
`UCASE(str/column_name)`.

5. The correct output of
`mysql>SELECT TRIM(LEADING '&' FROM '&&& India &&& ');`
   (a) India &&   (b) India &&&
   (c) && India   (d) &&& India

Ans. (b) This function is used to return a string after removing all prefix or suffix spaces from the given string. In other words, this function removes leading and trailing spaces from a given string. LEADING indicates only the leading prefixes are to be removed.

6. The default date format is
   (a) MM-DD-YYYY   (b) YYYY-MM-DD
   (c) DD-MM-YYYY   (d) None of these

Ans. (b) The default format for dates in MySQL is fixed as YYYY-MM-DD and we have to follow that.

7. Which of the following function returns an integer that indicates the position of the first occurrence of the sub-string within the string?
   (a) INSTR( )   (b) RTRIM( )
   (c) LENGTH( )   (d) TRIM( )

Ans. (a) The syntax of the INSTR function is
`INSTR(ori_str/column_name,sub_str)`
where, ori_str is the string to be searched and sub_str is the string to be searched from ori_str.

8. Write the output of the following SQL command.
`SELECT ROUND (47.89);`
   (a) 47.88   (b) 47.8
   (c) 48.0   (d) 50

Ans. (c) The ROUND() function rounds up the number to the upwards or downwards to the nearest whole number.

9. Which of the following function returns the name of the month from selected date?
   (a) MONTH(date)
   (b) MONTH_NAME(date)
   (c) MONTHNAME(date)
   (d) NAME_MONTH()

Ans. (c) `mysql> SELECT MONTHNAME ('2021-09-30');`
Above query produces the following output:

```
+----------------------+
| MONTHNAME('2021-09-30') |
+----------------------+
| September            |
+----------------------+
```

10. Which of the following function returns only the day number from month of selected date?

(a) DAY(date)

(b) DAYNO(date)

(c) DAY_NUMBER(date)

(d) DATE(date)

Ans. (*a*) `mysql> SELECT DAY('2021-09-30');`

Above query produces the following output:

```
+--------------------+
| DAY('2021-09-30')  |
+--------------------+
|              30    |
+--------------------+
```

11. What will be returned by the given query?

```
SELECT ROUND(153.669,2);
```

(a) 153.6   (b) 153.66

(c) 153.67   (d) 153.7

Ans. (*c*)ROUND() function will round off the decimal places up to 2 places.

12. What will be returned by the given query ?

```
SELECT INSTR('INDIA', 'DI');
```

(a) 2   (b) 3

(c) −2   (d) −3

Ans. (*b*) INSTR function returns the starting index of the substring that is passed as second argument in the function.

• Case Based MCQs

13. Shanya Kumar is working with the following table Customers:

Table : Customers

CNO	CNAME	CITIES
C1	SANYAM	DELHI
C2	SHRUTI	DELHI
C3	MEHER	MUMBAI
C4	SAKSHI	CHENNAI
C5	RITESH	INDORE
C6	RAHUL	DELHI
C7	AMEER	CHENNAI
C8	MINAKSHI	BANGLORE
C9	ANSHUL	MUMBAI

She has been given some queries to develop . Help her to achieve the task.

Shanya Kumar is working with the following table Customers : (Put the table)

She has been given some queries to develop. Help her to achieve the task.

(i) Choose the correct query to display the length of customer's name.

(a) `mysql>SELECT LENGTH(CNAME) FROM Customers;`

(b) `mysql>SELECT LEN(CNAME) FROM Customers;`

(c) `mysql>SELECT COUNT(NAME) FROM Customers;`

(d) `mysql>SELECT COUNT(CNAME) FROM Customers;`

(ii) Choose the correct query to display the city names in lower case letter whose CNO is either C5 or C9.

(a) `mysql>SELECT UPPERCASE(CITIES)FROM Customers WHERE CNO ='C5' OR CNO ='C9'`

(b) `mysql>SELECT UPPER(CITIES)FROM Customers WHERE CNO ='C5' OR 'C9'`

(c) `mysql>SELECT UPPER(CITIES)FROM Customers WHERE CNO ='C5' OR CNO ='C9'`

(d) `mysql>SELECT UPPER(CITIES)FROM Customers WHERE CNO IS EITHER 'C5' OR 'C9'`

(iii) Choose the correct query to display the length of customer's name for those customers whose name end with R or L.

(a) `mysql>SELECT LEN(CNAME)FROM Customers WHERE CNAME LIKE '%R' OR CNAME LIKE '%L';`

(b) `mysql>SELECT LENGTH(CNAME)FROM Customers WHERE CNAME LIKE '%R' OR CNAME LIKE '%L';`

(c) `mysql>SELECT LENGTH(CNAME)FROM Customers WHERE CNAME = '%R' OR CNAME = '%L';`

(d) `mysql>SELECT LENGTH(CNAME)FROM Customers WHERE CNAME LIKE '%R' OR LIKE '%L';`

(iv) Choose the correct query to display the Customer's name and their respective cities merged together for all the customers whose CNO is ending with 8.

(a) `mysql>SELECT MERGE(CNAME,CITIES) Customers WHERE CNO LIKE '%8';`

(b) `mysql>SELECT CNAME,CITIES FROM Customers WHERE CNO LIKE '%8';`

(c) `mysql>SELECT CONCAT(CNAME,CITIES) Customers WHERE CNO = '%8';`

(d) `mysql>SELECT CONCAT(CNAME,CITIES) FROM Customers WHERE CNO LIKE '%8';`

(v) Choose the correct query to display the left most 4 letters from the customers who lives in Mumbai or Banglore.

(a) `mysql>SELECT LEFT(CNAME)FROM Customers WHERE CITIES ='MUMBAI' OR CITIES = 'BANGLORE';`

(b) `mysql>SELECT LEFT(CNAME,3)FROM Customers WHERE CITIES ='MUMBAI' OR CITIES = 'BANGLORE';`

(c) `mysql>SELECT LEFT(CNAME,4)FROM Customers WHERE CITIES ='MUMBAI' OR 'BANGLORE';`

(d) `mysql>SELECT LEFT(CNAME,4)FROM Customers WHERE CITIES ='MUMBAI' OR CITIES = 'BANGLORE';`

Ans. (i) (a) `mysql>SELECT LENGTH(CNAME) FROM Customers;`

(ii) (c) `mysql>SELECT UPPER(CITIES)FROM Customers WHERE CNO ='C5' OR CNO ='C9'`

(iii) (b) `mysql>SELECT LENGTH(CNAME)FROM Customers WHERE CNAME IIKE '%R' OR CNAME LIKE '%L';`

(iv) (c) `mysql>SELECT CONCAT(CNAME,CITIES) FROM Customers WHERE CNO LIKE '%8';`

(v) (d) `mysql>SELECT LEFT(CNAME,4)FROM Customers WHERE CITIES ='MUMBAI' OR CITIES = 'BANGLORE';`

PART 2
Subjective Questions

• Short Answer Type Questions

1. Which type of MySQL function accepts only numeric values? Give the name of some functions of that type.

Ans. Mathematical functions accept only numeric values and return the value of same type. These functions are used to perform mathematical operations on the database data.

Some mathematical functions are

POW()/POWER(), ROUND(), etc.

2. Which SQL function is used to remove leading and trailing spaces from a character expression X, where X = 'LEARNING ###MYSQL####' (# denotes a blank space) and also give the output of X.

Ans. TRIM function is used to remove all leading and trailing spaces from the given character expression.

Syntax `TRIM([{BOTH|LEADING|TRAILING} [remstr] FROM] str/column_name)`

e.g. `mysql> SELECT TRIM(' LEARNING ###MYSQL#### ');`

Output `LEARNING###MYSQL`

Spaces between 'LEARNING' and 'MYSQL' cannot be removed.

3. Write the output of following MySQL queries:

(i) `SELECT ROUND(6.5675,2);`

(ii) `SELECT TRUNCATE(5.3456,2);`

(iii) `SELECT DAYOFMONTH(curdate());`

(iv) `SELECT MID('PRE_BOARDCLASS 12',4,6);`

Ans. (i)

```
+-------------------+
| ROUND (6.5675,2)  |
+-------------------+
| 6.57              |
+-------------------+
```

(ii)

```
+-------------------+
| TRUNCATE(5.3456.2)|
+-------------------+
| 5.34              |
+-------------------+
```

(iii) If curdate is 05/12/2017, then output is 5.

(iv)

```
+-------------------------------+
| MID('PRE_BOARDCLASS 12',4,6)  |
+-------------------------------+
| _BOARD                        |
+-------------------------------+
```

4. Mr. Manav, a database administrator in "Global Educational and Training Institute" has created following table named "Training" for the upcoming training schedule:

Table : Training

Training_Id	Name	Email_Id	Topic	City	Fee
ND01	Mr. Rajan	raj@gmail. com	Cyber Security	New Delhi	10000
GU01	Ms. Urvashi	urv@yahoo.com	ICT in Education	Gurugram	15000
FD01	Ms. Neena	neenarediff.com	Cyber Security	Faridabad	12000
ND02	Mr. Vinay	NULL	ICT in Education	New Delhi	13000
GU02	Mr. Naveen	nav@gmail.com	Cyber Security	Gurugram	NULL

Predict the output of the following queries:

(i) `SELECT SUBSTR(City,2,4) FROM Training WHERE Topic <> 'Cyber Security';`

(ii) `SELECT NAME FROM Training WHERE INSTR (Email_Id, '@')=0;`

Ans. (i)

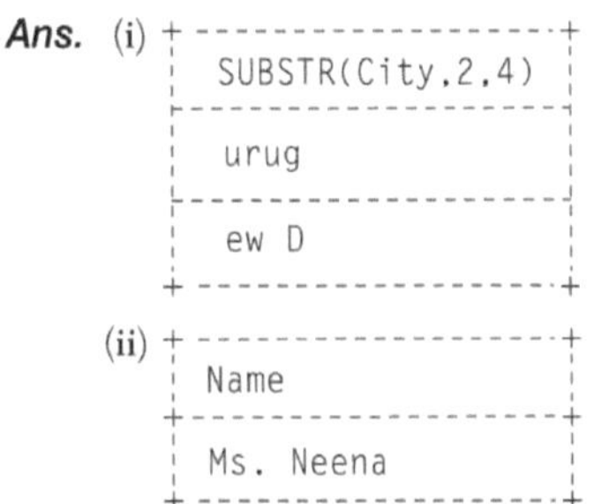

```
+-----------------+
| SUBSTR(City,2,4)|
+-----------------+
| urug            |
+-----------------+
| ew D            |
+-----------------+
```

(ii)

```
+-------------+
| Name        |
+-------------+
| Ms. Neena   |
+-------------+
```

5. Which function is used to display the position of occurrence of a string 'OUR' in string 'COURSE'? Explain.

Ans. The INSTR function searches for given second string into the first string and returns the position.

Syntax `INSTR(str1,str2)`

e.g. `mysql>SELECT INSTR('COURSE','OUR');`

The output will be 2 because the position of string 'OUR' is at 2 in the given string 'COURSE'.

6. Predict the output of the following queries:

(i) `mysql>SELECT POWER(3,2);`

(ii) `mysql>SELECT DATE('2009-01-21 02:01:04');`

Ans. (i)
```
+-------------------+
|  POWER (3,2)      |
+-------------------+
|  9                |
+-------------------+
```

(ii)
```
+-----------------------------+
| DATE('2009-01-21 02:01:04') |
+-----------------------------+
| 2009-01-21                  |
+-----------------------------+
```

7. Write the output of the following queries:

(i) `mysql>SELECT POWER(-6,3);`

(ii) `mysql>SELECT YEAR('2014-02-04');`

Ans. (i)
```
+-------------------+
|  POWER (-6,3)     |
+-------------------+
|  -216             |
+-------------------+
```

(ii)
```
+-------------------+
| YEAR ('2014-02-04')|
+-------------------+
|  2014             |
+-------------------+
```

8. Write the output of the following queries:

(i) `mysql>SELECT LENGTH('Name');`

(ii) `mysql>SELECT MID('information',3,2);`

Ans. (i)
```
+-------------------+
| LENGTH ('Name')   |
+-------------------+
|  4                |
+-------------------+
```

(ii)
```
+-------------------------+
| MID ('information'3,2)  |
+-------------------------+
|  fo                     |
+-------------------------+
```

9. Write the output of the following query:

`mysql>SELECT SUBSTR('STUDENT',3,3);`

Ans.

```
+-------------------------+
| SUBSTR('STUDENT',3,3)   |
+-------------------------+
|  UDE                    |
+-------------------------+
```

10. Consider the following table structure :

STUDENT (RollNo, Name, Class, Stream, Percentage)

Give the answer of the following questions on the basis of the above table structure.

(i) Write a query to display the 3rd to 7th character of name attribute.

(ii) Write a query to display the name of each student in uppercase letters with their RollNo, whose percentage is greater than 70.

Ans. (i) `mysql>SELECT SUBSTR(Name,3,5) FROM STUDENT;`

(ii) `mysql> SELECT UCASE(Name), RollNo FROM STUDENT WHERE Percentage>70;`

11. What is the differences between the string function and numeric function ?

Ans. Differences between string and numeric functions are given below:

String Function	Numeric Function
Accepts text input.	Accepts only numeric values.
Returns both numeric and string values.	Returns only numeric values.
String functions include ASCII(), CHAR(), LEFT(), etc.	Numeric functions include POW(), ROUND (), TRUNCATE(), etc.

12. Mention the type of the functions given below with their purpose.

(i) TRUNCATE( )

(ii) DAYOFMONTH( )

(iii) LEFT( )

Ans. (i) **TRUNCATE**( ) It is a mathematical function and returns a number truncated upto specified number of digits.

(ii) **DAYOFMONTH**( ) It is a Date/Time function and returns the day of month for the specified date.

(iii) **LEFT**( ) It is a string function and returns the leftmost number of characters as specified.

13. Give the output of following commands :

(i) `mysql>SELECT LEFT ('Swati',4);`

(ii) `mysql>SELECT RTRIM ('!!!!!Study is important!!!!!');`

(iii) `mysql>SELECT ROUND(3234.343,1);`

where, !!!!! denotes blank spaces.

Ans. (i)
```
+-------------------+
|  LEFT ('Swati', 4)|
+-------------------+
|  Swat             |
+-------------------+
```

(ii)
```
+-------------------------------------------+
| RTRIM('!!!!! Study is important !!!!!')   |
+-------------------------------------------+
| !!!!! Study is important                  |
+-------------------------------------------+
```

(iii)
```
+-------------------+
|  ROUND (3234.343,1)|
+-------------------+
|  3234.3           |
+-------------------+
```

14. Write the output of the following SQL queries:

(i) `SELECT SUBSTR(TRIM(' INDIA Is Great ',3,6) ;`

(ii) `SELECT ROUND(654.67152) + ROUND(152.4146,2) ;`

(iii) `SELECT INSTR('MOBILE PHONE','E') ;`

(iv) `SELECT DAYOFMONTH('2019-11-22');`

Ans. (i)
```
+------------------------------------------+
| SUBSTR (TRIM (' INDIA Is Great ',3,6)    |
+------------------------------------------+
| DIA Is                                   |
+------------------------------------------+
```

(ii)
```
+------------------------------------------+
| ROUND(654.67152)+ ROUND(152.4146,2)      |
+------------------------------------------+
| 807.41                                   |
+------------------------------------------+
```

(iii)
```
+------------------------------------------+
| INSTR ('MOBILE PHONE', 'E')              |
+------------------------------------------+
| 6                                        |
+------------------------------------------+
```

(iv)
```
+------------------------------------------+
| DAYOFMONTH ('2019-11-22')                |
+------------------------------------------+
| 22                                       |
+------------------------------------------+
```

15. Wrtie any four differences between single-row functions and multiple-row functions. **[NCERT]**

Ans.

Single-row functions	Multiple-row functions / Aggregate functions
It operates on a single row at a time.	It operates on multiple rows.
It returns one result per row.	It returns one result for multiple rows.
It can be used in SELECT, WHERE and ORDER BY clause.	It can be used in the SELECT clause only.
Mathematical, String and Date functions are examples of single-row functions.	MAX(), MIN(), AVG(), SUM(), COUNT() and COUNT(*) are examples of multiple-row functions.

16. Write the name of the functions to perform the following operations: **[NCERT]**

(i) To display the day like "Monday", "Tuesday", from the date when India got independence.

(ii) To display the specified number of characters from a particular position of the given string.

(iii) To display the name of the month in which you were born.

(iv) To display your name in capital letters.

Ans. (i) DAYNAME( )

(ii) MID( ) or SUBSTR( ) or SUBSTRING( )

(iii) MONTHNAME( )

(iv) UPPER( ) or UCASE( )

• Long Answer Type Questions

17. Write the output produced by the following SQL commands: **[NCERT]**

(i) `SELECT POW(2,3);`

(ii) `SELECT ROUND(123.2345, 2), ROUND(342.9234,-1);`

(iii) `SELECT LENGTH("Informatics Practices");`

(iv) `SELECT YEAR("1979/11/26"), MONTH ("1979/11/26"), DAY("1979/11/26"), MONTHNAME("1979/11/26");`

(v) `SELECT LEFT("INDIA",3), RIGHT("Computer Science",4);`

(vi) `SELECT MID("Informatics",3,4), SUBSTR("Practices",3);`

Ans. (i)
```
+--------+
| POW(2,3)|
+--------+
| 8      |
+--------+
```

(ii)
```
+-------------------------------------+
| ROUND(123.2345,2),ROUND(342.9234,-1)|
+-------------------------------------+
| 123.23  343.0                       |
+-------------------------------------+
```

(iii)
```
+-------------------------------+
| LENGTH("Informatics Practices")|
+-------------------------------+
| 21                            |
+-------------------------------+
```

(iv)
```
+-----------------------------------------------+
| YEAR("1979/11/26"),MONTH("1979/11/26"),        |
| DAY("1979/11/26"),MONTHNAME("1979/11/26")      |
+-----------------------------------------------+
| 1979   11   26   November                     |
+-----------------------------------------------+
```

(v)
```
+-----------------------------------------------+
| LEFT("INDIA",3),RIGHT("Computer Science",4)   |
+-----------------------------------------------+
| IND  ence                                     |
+-----------------------------------------------+
```

(vi)
```
+-----------------------------------------------+
| MID("Informatics",3,4),SUBSTR("Practices",3)  |
+-----------------------------------------------+
| Form  actices                                 |
+-----------------------------------------------+
```

18. Consider the following table Club :

Table : Club

COACH_ID	COACH NAME	AGE	SPORTS	Date_of_Joining	PAY
1	Rajesh	30	Karate	1999-08-25	1000
2	Anuj	35	Swimming	2000-01-05	750
3	Shuchi	25	Basketball	2005-01-04	1200
4	Reetika	28	Badminton	2002-08-25	1400
5	Virendra	32	Cricket	1996-05-17	1500

Give the answer of the following questions on the basis of the above table.

(i) Write a query to display the substring of 4 characters of the name of each coach, starting from second character, with their age.

(ii) What will be the output of the following query?

```
mysql>SELECT LENGTH(COACHNAME) FROM Club
WHERE AGE>30;
```

(iii) Write a query to display the day for the Date_of_Joining column.

(iv) What will be the output of the following query?

```
mysql>SELECT PAY*0.25+1000
FROM Club
WHERE COACHNAME LIKE 'R%';
```

(v) Write a query to display 3 characters from left of coach name.

Ans. (i) `mysql>SELECT SUBSTR (COACHNAME,2,4) , AGE FROM Club;`

(ii) 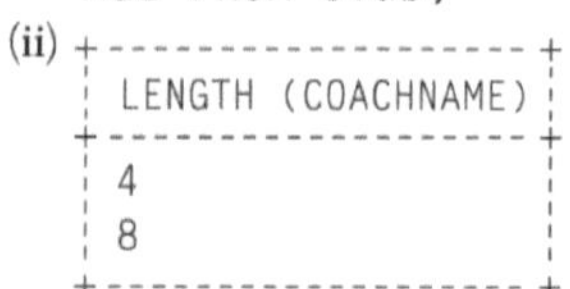
```
+---------------------+
| LENGTH (COACHNAME)  |
+---------------------+
| 4                   |
| 8                   |
+---------------------+
```

(iii) `mysql>SELECT DAY(Date_of_Joining);`

(iv) 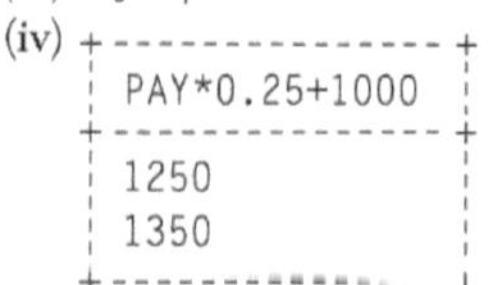
```
+---------------------+
| PAY*0.25+1000       |
+---------------------+
| 1250                |
| 1350                |
+---------------------+
```

(v) `SELECT LEFT (COACHNAME,3) FROM Club;`

19. Write SQL commands for (i) to (iii) and write the output for (iv) on the basis of table Graduate.

Table : Graduate

SNo	Name	Stipend	Subject	Average	Div
1	Karan	400	Physics	68	1
2	Divakar	450	Computers	68	1
3	Divya	300	Chemistry	62	2
4	Arun	350	Physics	63	1
5	Sabina	500	Mathematics	70	1
6	John	400	Chemistry	55	2
7	Robert	250	Physics	64	1
8	Rubina	450	Mathematics	68	1
9	Vikas	500	Computers	62	1
10	Mohan	300	Mathematics	57	2

(i) List the names of those students who obtained Div 1.

(ii) Display a report, listing Name , Stipend , Subject and amount of stipend received in a year assuming that the Stipend is paid every month.

(iii) To insert a new row in the Graduate table :

11,"KAJOL",300, "COMPUTERS",75,1

(iv) Give the output of the following SQL statement based on table Graduate:

(a) `SELECT LEFT(NAME,3) FROM Graduate WHERE SNO>7;`

(b) `SELECT Name, Stipend FROM Graduate WHERE Subject="Chemistry" OR Subject="Physics";`

(c) `SELECT * FROM Graduate WHERE Subject LIKE 'C%' AND Average=68;`

(d) `SELECT Name FROM Graduate WHERE DIV=2;`

Ans. (i) `SELECT Name FROM Graduate WHERE Div=1;`

(ii) `SELECT Name, Stipend, Subject, Stipend *12 FROM Graduate;`

(iii) `INSERT INTO Graduate VALUES (11, 'Kajol', 300, 'Computers', 75,1);`

(iv) (a)
```
+-----------------+
| LEFT(NAME,3)    |
+-----------------+
| Rub             |
| Vik             |
| Moh             |
+-----------------+
```

(b)
```
+---------+---------+
| Name    | Stipend |
+---------+---------+
| Karan   | 400     |
| Divya   | 300     |
| Arun    | 350     |
| John    | 400     |
| Robert  | 250     |
+---------+---------+
```

(c)
```
+-----+---------+---------+-----------+---------+-----+
| SNO | Name    | Stipend | Subject   | Average | Div |
+-----+---------+---------+-----------+---------+-----+
| 2   | Divakar | 450     | Computers | 68      | 1   |
+-----+---------+---------+-----------+---------+-----+
```

(d)
```
+-------+
| Name  |
+-------+
| Divya |
| John  |
| Mohan |
+-------+
```

20. Write SQL commands for (i) to (v) and write the output for (vi) on the basis of table Furniture.

Table : Furniture

No	Itemname	Type	Dateofstock	Price	Discount
1	White lotus	Double Bed	23/02/02	30000	25
2	Pink feather	Baby Cot	20/01/02	7000	20
3	Dolphin	Baby Cot	19/02/02	9500	20
4	Decent	Office Table	01/01/02	25000	30
5	Comfort Zone	Double Bed	12/01/02	25000	25
6	Donald	Baby Cot	24/02/02	6500	15
7	Royal finish	Office Table	20/02/02	18000	30
8	Royal tiger	Sofa	22/02/02	31000	30
9	Econo sitting	Sofa	13/12/01	9500	25
10	Eating paradise	Dining Table	19/02/02	11500	25
11	WoodComfort	Double Bed	23/03/03	25000	25
12	Old Fox	Sofa	20/02/03	17000	20
13	Micky	Baby Cot	21/02/03	7500	15

(i) To show all information about the baby cots from the Furniture table.

(ii) To list the itemname which are priced at more than 15000 from the Furniture table.

(iii) To list itemname and type of those items, in which date of stock is before 22/01/02 from the Furniture table in the descending order of itemname.

(iv) To display itemname and dataofstock of those items, whose type is " Sofa" from Furniture table.

(v) To insert a new row in the Furniture table with the following data:

14,"Velvet touch" , "Double Bed",{25/03/03}, 25000,30

(vi) Give the output of the following SQL statement based on table Furniture.

(a) `SELECT LEFT(Itemname,3) FROM Furniture WHERE Type="Double Bed";`

(b) `SELECT MONTHNAME(Dateofstock) FROM Furniture WHERE Type="Sofa";`

(c) `SELECT * FROM Furniture WHERE Itemname LIKE 'E%';`

(d) `SELECT Price*Discount FROM Furniture WHERE Dateofstock>31/12/02;`

Ans. (i)
```
SELECT  *  FROM  Furniture  WHERE  Type=
"Baby Cot";
```

(ii)
```
SELECT  Itemname  FROM  Furniture  WHERE
Price>15000;
```

(iii)
```
SELECT  Itemname,  Type  FROM  Furniture
WHERE  Dateofstock < "22/01/02" ORDER BY
Itemname DESC;
```

(iv)
```
SELECT  Itemname  ,  Dateofstock  FROM
Furniture WHERE Type= 'Sofa';
```

(v)
```
INSERT   INTO   Furniture   VALUES   (14,
'Velvet     touch',     'Double     Bed',
"25/03/03", 25000, 30);
```

(vi) (a)
```
+------------------+
| LEFT(Itemane,3)  |
+------------------+
| whi              |
+------------------+
| Com              |
+------------------+
| Woo              |
+------------------+
```

(b)
```
+------------------------+
| MONTHNAME(Dateofstock) |
+------------------------+
| February               |
+------------------------+
| December               |
+------------------------+
| February               |
+------------------------+
```

(c)
```
+----+---------+-------+-------------+-------+----------+
| NO | IterName| Type  | Dateofstock | Price | Dsicount |
+----+---------+-------+-------------+-------+----------+
| 9  | Econo   | Sofa  | 13/12/01    | 9500  | 25       |
|    | sitting |       |             |       |          |
+----+---------+-------+-------------+-------+----------+
| 10 | Eating  | Dining| 19/02/02    | 11500 | 25       |
|    | paradise| Table |             |       |          |
+----+---------+-------+-------------+-------+----------+
```

(d)
```
+---------------+
| Price*DIscount |
+---------------+
| 625000        |
+---------------+
| 340000        |
+---------------+
| 112500        |
+---------------+
```

21. Consider the following table named "Product", showing details of products being sold in a grocery shop.

Table : Product

PCode	PName	UPrice	Manufacture
P01	Washing Powder	120	Surf
P02	Tooth Paste	54	Colgate
P03	Soap	25	Lux
P04	Tooth Paste	65	Pepsodent
P05	Soap	38	Dove
P06	Shampoo	245	Dove

Write SQL queries for the following and output(s) produced by executing the following queries on the basis of the information given above in the table Product.

(i) Create the table Product with appropriate data types and constraints.

(ii) Identify the primary key in table Product.

(iii) List the product code, product name and price in with their product name for all Dove manufacture.

(iv) Increase the price by 12 per cent for all the products manufactured by Dove.

Ans. (i)
```
CREATE TABLE Product(
PCode char(3) PRIMARY KEY,
PName varchar(25) NOT NULL,
UPrice int(4),
Manufacture varchar(30));
```

(ii) PCode

(iii)
```
SELECT PCode,PName, UPrice FROM Product
WHERE Manufacture="Dove";
```

(iv)
```
UPDATE  Product  SET  UPrice
=UPrice+0.12*UPrice  WHERE
Manufacture="Dove";
```

22. Given the following table Employee :

Table : Employee

No.	Name	Age	Department	Dateofrtd	Salary	Sex
1	Pankaj	54	Engg.	10/01/97	1200	M
2	Shalini	41	Estbl.	24/03/98	2000	F
3	Sanjay	32	Engg.	12/12/96	3500	M
4	Sudha	25	Science	01/07/99	4700	F
5	Rakesh	32	Engg.	05/09/97	2500	M
6	Shakeel	40	Language	27/06/98	3000	M
7	Surya	44	Estbl.	25/02/97	2100	M
8	Shikha	33	Science	31/07/97	2600	F

Write SQL commands for (i) to (v).

(i) To show all information about the employees of Engg. branch.

(ii) To list the names of female employees who are in Science branch.

(iii) To list the names of all employees with their date of retirement in ascending order.

(iv) To display employee's name , salary , age for male employees only.

(v) To insert a new row in the Employee table with the following data:

9,"Rohit",46,"Language",{22/06/98},2300,"M"

Ans. (i)
```
SELECT * FROM Employee WHERE Branch=
'Engg.';
```
(ii)
```
SELECT Name FROM Employee WHERE Sex= 'F'
AND Department= 'Science';
```
(iii)
```
SELECT Name, Dateofrtd FROM Employee
ORDER BY Dateofrtd;
```
(iv)
```
SELECT Name, Salary, Age FROM Employee
WHERE Sex= 'M';
```
(v)
```
INSERT INTO Employee VALUES (9, 'Rohit',
46, 'Language',"22/06/98",2300, 'M');
```

23. Consider the following table WORKER and answer (i) and (ii) parts of this question.

Table : Worker

Ecode	Name	Desig	Plevel	DOJ	DOB
11	Radhey Shyam	Supervisor	P001	13-Sep-2004	23-Aug-1981
12	Chander Nath	Operator	P003	22-Feb-2010	12-Jul-1987
13	Fizza	Operator	P003	14-June-2009	14-Oct-1983
15	Ameen Ahmed	Mechanic	P002	21-Aug-2006	13-Mar-1984
18	Sanya	Clerk	P002	19-Dec-2005	09-June-1983

(i) Write SQL commands for the following statements:

(a) To display the details of all workers in descending order of DOB.

(b) To display Name and Desig of those workers whose Plevel is either P001 or P002.

(c) To display the content of all the workers, whose DOB is in between '19-JAN-1984' and '18-JAN-1987'.

(d) To add a new row with the following:

19, 'Daya kishore', 'Operator', 'P003', '19-Jun-2008', '11-Jul-1984'

(ii) Give the output of the following SQL queries:

(a)
```
SELECT Desig,Plevel FROM Worker WHERE
Desig LIKE '%or';
```
(b)
```
SELECT RIGHT(Name,3) FROM Worker WHERE
Plevel='P002';
```
(c)
```
SELECT YEAR(DOJ) FROM Worker;
```

Ans. (i) (a)
```
SELECT * FROM Worker ORDER BY DOB
DESC;
```
(b)
```
SELECT Name, Desig FROM Worker WHERE
Plevel IN ("P001", "P002");
```
(c)
```
SELECT * FROM Worker WHERE DOB BETWEEN
"19-JAN-1984" AND "18-JAN-1987";
```
(d)
```
INSERT INTO Worker VALUES
(19, 'Daya kishore', 'Operator',
'P003','19-Jun-2008', '11-Jul-1984');
```

(ii) (a)
```
+-----------+--------+
| Desig     | Plevel |
+-----------+--------+
| Supervisor| P001   |
| Operator  | P003   |
| Operator  | P003   |
+-----------+--------+
```
(b)
```
+--------------+
| RIGHT(Name,3)|
+--------------+
| med          |
+--------------+
| nya          |
+--------------+
```
(c)
```
+-----------+
| YEAR(DOJ) |
+-----------+
| 2004      |
+-----------+
| 2009      |
+-----------+
| 2006      |
+-----------+
| 2005      |
+-----------+
```

24. Write the SQL functions which will perform the following operations:

(i) To display the name of the month of the current date.

(ii) To remove spaces from the beginning and end of a string " Panaroma ".

(iii) To display the name of the day e.g. Friday or Sunday from your date of birth, dob.

(iv) To display the starting position of your first name(fname) from your whole name (name).

(v) To compute the remainder of division between two numbers n1 and n2.

[CBSE SAMPLE PAPER 2020]

Ans. (i) MONTHNAME(date(now()))

(ii) TRIM (" Panaroma ")

(iii) DAYNAME(date(dob))

(iv) INSTR(name, fname)

(v) MOD(n1,n2)

25. Consider a table Salesman with the following data:

Table : Salesman

SNO	SNAME	SALARY	BONUS	DATE_OF_JOIN
A01	Beena Mehta	30000	45.23	29-10-2019
A02	K. L. Sahay	50000	25.34	13-03-2018
B03	Nisha Thakkar	30000	35.00	18-03-2017
B04	Leela Yadav	80000	NULL	31-12-2018
C05	Gautam Gola	20000	NULL	23-01-1989
C06	Trapti Garg	70000	12.37	15-06-1987
D07	Neena Sharma	50000	27.89	18-03-1999

Write SQL queries using SQL functions to perform the following operations:

(i) Display salesman name and bonus after rounding off to zero decimal places.

(ii) Display the position of occurrence of the string "ta" in salesman names.

(iii) Display the four characters from salesman name starting from second character.

(iv) Display the month name for the date of join of salesman.

(v) Display the name of the weekday for the date of join of salesman.

Ans.

(i)
```
SELECT SNAME, ROUND(BONUS,0) FROM
Salesman;
```

(ii)
```
SELECT INSTR(SNAME, "ta") FROM Salesman;
```

(iii)
```
SELECT MID(SNAME,2,4) FROM Salesman;
```
or
```
SELECT SUBSTRING(SNAME,2,4) FROM
Salesman;
```

(iv)
```
SELECT MONTHNAME(DATE_OF_JOIN) FROM
Salesman;
```

(v)
```
SELECT DAYNAME(DATE_OF_JOIN) FROM
Salesman;
```

Chapter Test

Multiple Choice Questions

1. Which of the following performs a pre-defined task and returns some type of result?
    (a) Database   (b) SQL function
    (c) Implementation   (d) None of these

2. Which SQL function remove the leading blank spaces from a string ?
    (a) CHAR( )   (b) CONCAT( )
    (c) LCASE( )   (d) LTRIM( )

3. Which of the following function returns the value of a number raised to the power of another number?
    (a) ROUND( )   (b) POWER( )
    (c) POW( )   (d) Both (b) and (c)

4. Which of the following function returns only date part from the given date/time argument?
    (a) DATE( )   (b) CURDATE( )
    (c) DATECUR( )   (d) None of these

5. Identify single-row functions of MySQL amongst the following.
    (a) TRIM()   (b) MAX()
    (c) ROUND()   (d) Both (a) and (c)

Short Answer Type Questions

6. Write the output of the following SQL queries:
    (i) SELECT INSTR('INTERNATIONAL', 'NA');
    (ii) SELECT LENGTH(MID('NETWORK',2,3));
    (iii) SELECT ROUND(563.345,–2);
    (iv) SELECT DAYOFYEAR('2014-01-30');

7. State differences between date functions NOW( ) and DAY( ) of MySQL.

Long Answer Type Questions

8. Write SQL command for questions (i) to (v) on the basis of table Teacher.

Table: Teacher

No	Name	Department	Dateofjoining	Salary	Sex
1	Raja	Computer	21/05/98	8000	M
2	Sangita	History	21/05/97	9000	F
3	Ritu	Sociology	29/08/98	8000	F
4	Kumar	Linguistics	13/06/96	10000	M
5	Venkat	History	31/10/99	8000	M
6	Sidhu	Computer	21/05/86	14000	M
7	Aishwarya	Sociology	11/01/88	12000	F

    (i) To select all the information of teacher in computer department.
    (ii) To list the name of female teachers in History department.
    (iii) To list all names of teachers with date of admission in ascending order.
    (iv) To display teacher's Name, Department and Salary of female teacher.
    (v) To insert a new record in the Teacher table with the following data:
        8,"Mersha","Computer", '01/01/2000',12000,"M"

9. Write SQL command for questions (i) to (v) on the basis of table Interiors.

Table : Interiors

No	Itemname	Type	Dateofstock	Price	Discount
1	Red_rose	Double Bed	23/02/02	32000	15
2	Soft touch	Baby Cot	20/01/02	9000	10
3	Jerry's home	Baby Cot	19/02/02	8500	10
4	Rough wood	Office Table	01/01/02	20000	20
5	Comfort zone	Double Bed	12/01/02	15000	20
6	Jerry look	Baby Cot	24/02/02	7000	19
7	Lion king	Office Table	20/02/02	16000	20
8	Royal tiger	Sofa	22/02/02	30000	25
9	Park sitting	Sofa	13/12/01	9000	15
10	Dine Paradise	Dining Table	19/02/02	11000	15
11	White wood	Double Bed	23/03/03	20000	20
12	James 007	Sofa	20/02/03	15000	15
13	Tom look	Baby Cot	21/02/03	7000	10

(i) To show all information about the sofas from the Interiors table.

(ii) To list the itemname which are priced at more than 10000 from the Interiors table.

(iii) To list Itemname and Type of those items, in which Dateofstock is be 22/01/02 from the Interiors table in descending order of Itemname.

(iv) To display Itemname and Dateofstock of items whose discount is more than 15.

(v) To insert a new row in the new one table with the following data:

    14," True Indian" , "Office Table",{28/03/03},15000,20

Answers

Multiple Choice Questions

1. (b)   2. (d)   3. (d)   4. (a)   5. (d)

For Detailed Solutions

Scan the code

Aggregate Functions and Querying

In this Chapter...

- ORDER BY Clause
- GROUP BY Clause
- HAVING Clause

Aggregate functions are also known as group functions, they return a result only in single row based on group of rows, rather than on single row. It always used with **SELECT** command and in **ORDER BY** and **HAVING** clauses.

SQL aggregate functions return a single value, calculated from values in a column.

Consider the following table Club:

Table : Club

Coachid	Coachname	Age	Sports	Dateofapp	Pay	Gender	City
1	Kukreja	35	Karate	1996-03-27	1000	M	Mumbai
2	Ravina	34	Karate	1998-01-29	12000	F	Chennai
3	Karan	34	Squash	1998-02-19	2000	M	Delhi
4	Tarun	33	Basketball	1998-01-01	1500	M	Delhi
5	Zubin	36	Swimming	1998-01-12	750	M	Delhi
6	Asha	32	Tennis	1996-09-23	900	Null	Delhi

AVG()

This function returns the average value of a specified column.

Syntax `SELECT AVG(column_name) FROM table_name;`

e.g.   Write a query to display the average pay of coaches.

```
mysql> SELECT AVG(Pay) FROM Club;
```

Above query produces the following output:

```
+-----------+
| AVG(Pay)  |
+-----------+
| 3025.0000 |
+-----------+
```

COUNT()

This function returns the total number of values or rows of the specified field or column. COUNT (*) is a special function, as it returns the count of all rows in a specified table. It includes all the null and duplicate values.

Syntax `SELECT COUNT(*) FROM table_name;`

e.g.   Write a query to display the total pay of all coaches.

```
mysql> SELECT COUNT(*) FROM Club;
```

Above query produces the following output:

```
+-----------+
| COUNT(*)  |
+-----------+
|    6      |
+-----------+
```

DISTINCT Keyword with COUNT() Function

The DISTINCT keyword helps us in removing the duplicates from the result. When it is used with aggregate function COUNT, it returns the number of distinct rows in a specified table.

Syntax `SELECT COUNT(DISTINCT column_name) FROM table_name;`

e.g. Write a query to display the number of coaches from table Club.

```
mysql>SELECT COUNT(DISTINCT Sports) FROM Club;
```

Above query produces the following output:

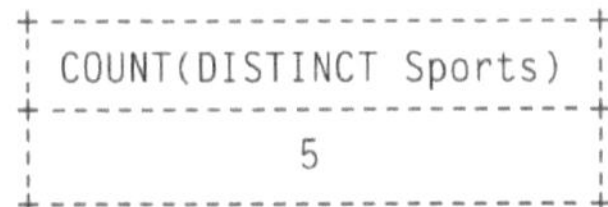

```
+------------------------+
| COUNT(DISTINCT Sports) |
+------------------------+
|           5            |
+------------------------+
```

MAX()

This function returns the largest value from the selected columns.

Syntax `SELECT MAX(column_name) FROM table_name;`

e.g. Write a query to display the maximam pay availed by the coaches.

```
mysql> SELECT MAX(Pay) FROM Club;
```

Above query produces the following output:

```
+-----------+
| MAX(Pay)  |
+-----------+
|   12000   |
+-----------+
```

MIN()

This function returns the smallest value from the selected column.

Syntax `SELECT MIN(column_name) FROM table_name;`

e.g. Write a query to display the minimum pay availed by the coaches.

```
mysql> SELECT MIN(Pay) FROM Club;
```

Above query produces the following output:

```
+-----------+
| MIN(Pay)  |
+-----------+
|    750    |
+-----------+
```

SUM()

This function returns the sum of values in the specified column. The SUM works on numeric fields only. Null values are excluded from the result returned.

Syntax `SELECT SUM(column_name) FROM table_name;`

e.g. Write a query to display the total pay of all coaches.

```
mysql> SELECT SUM(Pay) FROM Club;
```

Above query produces the following output:

```
+-----------+
| SUM(Pay)  |
+-----------+
|   18150   |
+-----------+
```

ORDER BY Clause

The ORDER BY clause is used to sort the result set along a specified column. The ORDER BY clause sorts the records in ascending order by default.

If you want to sort the records in descending order, you can use the DESC keyword.

Syntax
```
SELECT column_name(s)
     FROM table_name
     ORDER BY column_name(s) ASC/DESC;
```

Table: Persons

P_ID	LastName	FirstName	Address	City
1	Hansen	Ola	Timoteivn 10	Sandnes
2	Svendson	Tove	Borgvn 23	Sandnes
3	Pettersen	Kari	Storgt 20	Stavanger

Now, we want to select all the persons from the table Persons. However, we want to sort the persons by their last name in ascending order. We will use the following statement:

```
mysql>SELECT * FROM Persons ORDER BY
     LastName ASC;
```

The result set will look like this:

```
+------+-----------+-----------+--------------+------------+
| P_ID | LastName  | FirstName | Address      | City       |
+------+-----------+-----------+--------------+------------+
|  1   | Hansen    | Ola       | Timoteivn 10 | Sandness   |
|  3   | Pettersen | Kari      | Storgt 20    | Stavanger  |
|  2   | Svendson  | Tove      | Borgvn 23    | Sandnes    |
+------+-----------+-----------+--------------+------------+
```

GROUP BY Clause

The GROUP BY clause can be used with SELECT statement, if we want to select multiple records and group of results by one or more columns. AS keyword is optional and is used to assign a temporary name to the column or table.

Syntax
```
SELECT column1, column2
     FROM table_name
     WHERE [conditions]
     GROUP BY column1, column2
     ORDER BY column1, column2
```

Consider the following Employee table

Table : Employee

EmpID	EmpName	EmpEmail	PhoneNumber	Salary	City
1	Nidhi	nidhi@sam ple.com	9955669999	50000	Mumbai
2	Anay	anay@samp le.com	9875679861	55000	Pune
3	Rahul	rahul@sam ple.com	9876543212	35000	Delhi
4	Sonia	sonia@sam ple.com	9876543234	35000	Delhi
5	Akash	akash@sam ple.com	9866865686	25000	Mumbai

Write a query to retrieve the number of employees in each city.

```
SELECT COUNT(EmpID), City
FROM Employee
GROUP BY City;
```

This would produce the following result:

```
+-------------+--------+
| COUNT(EmpID) |  City  |
+-------------+--------+
|      2      | Delhi  |
|      2      | Mumbai |
|      1      | Pune   |
+-------------+--------+
```

Let's look at how to use the GROUP BY clause with the COUNT function in SQL.

In this example, we have a table called Products with the following data:

Table : Products

Product_id	Product_name	Category_id
1	Pear	50
2	Banana	50
3	Orange	50
4	Apple	50
5	Bread	75
6	Sliced Ham	25
7	Kleenex	NULL

Enter the following SQL statement:

```
SELECT Category_id, COUNT(*) AS
Total_products
FROM Products
WHERE Category_id IS NOT NULL
GROUP BY Category_id
ORDER BY Category_id;
```

There will be 3 records selected. These are the results that you should see:

```
+-------------+----------------+
| Category_id | Total_products |
+-------------+----------------+
|     25      |       1        |
|     50      |       4        |
|     75      |       1        |
+-------------+----------------+
```

HAVING Clause

The HAVING clause can be used only with the SELECT statement. HAVING is applied to summarised rows (summarised with GROUP BY). In which the completed data is firstly fetched and then separated according to condition. The HAVING clause was added to MySQL because the WHERE keyword could not be used with aggregate functions.

Syntax
```
SELECT column1, column2
FROM table1, table2
WHERE [ conditions ]
GROUP BY column1, column2
HAVING [ conditions ]
ORDER BY column1, column2
```

Consider the following table Order:

Table : Order

O_ID	OrderDate	OrderPrice	Customer
1	2015/01/23	1000	Rubeen
2	2014/11/15	1600	Sheena
3	2014/11/12	700	Jensen
4	2013/10/22	500	Rubeen
5	2013/10/16	2000	Jensen
6	2012/09/30	300	Sheena

```
mysql>SELECT Customer, SUM(OrderPrice)
FROM Order
GROUP BY Customer
HAVING  SUM(OrderPrice) <2000;
```

Above query produces the following output:

```
+----------+-----------------+
| Customer | SUM (OrderPrice) |
+----------+-----------------+
| Rubeen   |      1500        |
| Sheena   |      1900        |
+----------+-----------------+
```

Chapter Practice

Objective Questions

• Multiple Choice Questions

1. Which of the following is not an aggregate function?

(a) AVG()
(b) ADD()
(c) MAX()
(d) COUNT()

Ans. (*b*) There is no aggregate function named ADD() but SUM() is an aggregate function which performs mathematical sum of multiple rows having numerical values.

2. Which aggregate function returns the count of all rows in a specified table?

(a) SUM()
(b) DISTINCT()
(c) COUNT()
(d) None of these

Ans. (*c*) COUNT() function returns the total number of values or rows of the specified field or column.

3. In which function, NULL values are excluded from the result returned?

(a) SUM()
(b) MAX()
(c) MIN()
(d) All of these

Ans. (*d*) NULL values are excluded from the result returned by all the aggregate functions.

4. The AVG() function in MySQL is an example of

(a) Math function
(b) Text function
(c) Date function
(d) Aggregate function

Ans. (*d*) The AVG() function returns the average value from a column or multiple-rows.

So, the AVG ( ) function in MySQL is an example of aggregate function.

5. Which of the following function count all the values except NULL?

(a) COUNT(*)
(b) COUNT(column_name)
(c) COUNT(NOT NULL)
(d) COUNT(NULL)

Ans. (*a*) All aggregate functions exclude NULL values while performing the operation and COUNT(*) is an aggregate function.

6. What is the meaning of "GROUP BY" clause in MySQL?

(a) Group data by column values
(b) Group data by row values
(c) Group data by column and row values
(d) None of the mentioned

Ans. (*a*) Through GROUP BY clause we can create groups from a column of data in a table.

7. Which clause is similar to "HAVING" clause in MySQL?

(a) SELECT
(b) WHERE
(c) FROM
(d) None of the mentioned

Ans. (*b*) HAVING clause will act exactly same as WHERE clause. i.e. filtering the rows based on certain conditions.

8. Which clause is used with an "aggregate functions"?

(a) GROUP BY
(b) SELECT
(c) WHERE
(d) Both (a) and (c)

Ans. (*a*) "GROUP BY" is used with an aggregate functions.

9. What is the significance of the statement "GROUP BY d.name" in the following MySQL statement?

```
SELECT name, COUNT (emp_id), emp_no
FROM department
GROUP BY name;
```

(a) Counting of the field "name" on the table "department"
(b) Aggregation of the field "name" of table "department"
(c) Sorting of the field "name"
(d) None of the mentioned

Ans. (*b*) "GROUP BY" clause is used for aggregation of field. Above statement will find the aggregation of the field "name" of table "department".

10. What is the significance of the statement "HAVING COUNT (emp_id)>2" in the following MySQL statement?

```
SELECT name, COUNT (emp_id),emp_no
FROM department
GROUP BY name
HAVING COUNT (emp_id)>2;
```

(a) Filter out all rows whose total emp_id below 2
(b) Selecting those rows whose total emp_id>2
(c) Both (a) and (b)
(d) None of the mentioned

Ans. (*c*) "HAVING" clause are worked similar as "WHERE" clause i.e. filtering the rows based on certain conditions. GROUP BY command places conditions in the query using

HAVING clause. So, all the groups having employee count greater than 2 will be displayed.

11. What is the significance of "ORDER BY" in the following MySQL statement?

```
SELECT emp_id, fname, lname
FROM person
ORDER BY emp_id;
```

(a) Data of emp_id will be sorted
(b) Data of emp_id will be sorted in descending order
(c) Data of emp_id will be sorted in ascending order
(d) All of the mentioned

Ans. (c) Sorting in ascending or descending order depends on keyword "DESC" and "ASC". The default order is ascending.

12. What will be the order of sorting in the following MySQL statement?

```
SELECT emp_id, emp_name
FROM person
ORDER BY emp_id, emp_name;
```

(a) Sorting {emp_id, emp_name}
(b) Sorting {emp_name, emp_id}
(c) Sorting {emp_id} but not emp_name
(d) None of the mentioned

Ans. (a) In the query, first "emp_id" will be sorted then emp_name with respect to emp_id.

13. Which of the following is not a valid SQL statement?

(a) `SELECT MIN(pub_date) FROM books GROUP BY category HAVING pub_id = 4;`
(b) `SELECT MIN(pub_date) FROM books WHERE category = 'COOKING';`
(c) `SELECT COUNT(*) FROM orders WHERE customer# = 1005;`
(d) `SELECT MAX(COUNT(customer#)) FROM orders GROUP BY customer#;`

Ans. (a) HAVING clause is wrongly applied on attribute "pub_id" rather than attribute "category".

14. If emp_id contain the following set {9, 7, 6, 4, 3, 1, 2}, what will be the output on execution of the following MySQL statement?

```
SELECT emp_id
FROM person ORDER BY emp_id;
```

(a) {1, 2, 3, 4, 6, 7, 9}   (b) {2, 1, 4, 3, 7, 9, 6}
(c) {9, 7, 6, 4, 3, 1, 2}   (d) None of the mentioned

Ans. (a) "ORDER BY" clause sort the emp_id in the result set in ascending order and in absence of keyword ASC or DESC in the ORDER BY clause the default order is ascending.

15. Find odd one out?

(a) GROUP BY   (b) DESC
(c) ASC   (d) ORDER BY

Ans. (a) "ORDER BY", "DESC", "ASC" are related to sorting whereas "GROUP BY" is not related to sorting.

• Case Based MCQs

Direction *Read the case and answer the following questions.*

16. A School in Delhi uses database management system to store student details. The school maintains a database 'school_record' under which there are two tables.

Student Table Maintains general details about every student enrolled in school.

StuLibrary Table To store details of issued books. BookID is the unique identification number issued to each book. Minimum issue duration of a book is one day.   [CBSE Question Bank 2021]

Student	
Field	Type
StuID	numeric
StuName	varchar(20)
StuAddress	varchar(50)
StuFatherName	varchar(20)
StuContact	numeric
StuAadhar	numeric
	varchar(5)
StuSection	varchar(1)

StuLibrary	
Field	Type
BookID	numbric
StuID	numbric
Issued_date	Date
Return_date	Date

(i) Identify the SQL query which displays the data of StuLibrary table in ascending order of student ID.

I. `SELECT * FROM StuLibrary ORDER BY BookID;`

II. `SELECT * FROM StuLibrary ORDER BY StuID;`

III. `SELECT * FROM StuLibrary ORDER BY StuID ASC;`

IV. `SELECT * FROM StuLibrary ORDER BY StuID DESC;`

Choose the correct option, which displays the desired data.

(a) Both I and IV   (b) Both I and II
(c) Both III and IV   (d) Both II and III

Ans. (d) Since the default order of sorting is ASC or ascending, therefore if it is not mentioned in the query the query will take the default order.

(ii) The primary key for StuLibrary table is/are ....

(a) BookID   (b) BookID,StuID
(c) BookID,Issued_date (d) Issued_date

Ans. (a) Because BookID will have unique and NOT NULL values.

(iii) Which of the following SQL query will display dates on which number of issued books is greater than 5?

(a) `SELECT Issued_date FROM StuLibrary GROUP BY Issued_date WHERE COUNT(*)>5;`

(b) `SELECT Issued_date FROM StuLibrary GROUP BY Return_date HAVING COUNT(*)>5;`

(c) SELECT Issued_date FROM StuLibrary
GROUP BY Issued_date HAVING
COUNT(*)>5;
(d) SELECT Issued_date FROM StuLibrary
GROUP BY Return_date WHERE COUNT(*)>5;

Ans. (c) SELECT Issued_date FROM StuLibrary
GROUP BY Issued_date HAVING COUNT(*)>5;

17. **Table: Book_Information** **Table: Sales**

Column Name
Book_ID
Book_Title
Price

Column Name
Store_ID
Sales_Date
Sales_Amount

(i) Which SQL statement allows you to find the highest price from the table Book_Information?
(a) SELECT Book_ID,Book_Title,MAX(Price)
FROM Book_Information;
(b) SELECT MAX(Price) FROM Book_Information;
(c) SELECT MAXIMUM(Price) FROM
Book_Information;
(d) SELECT Price FROM Book_Information ORDER
BY Price DESC ;

Ans. (b) SELECT MAX(Price) FROM Book_Information;

(ii) Which SQL statement allows you to find sales amount for each store?
(a) SELECT Store_ID, SUM(Sales_Amount) FROM
Sales;
(b) SELECT Store_ID, SUM(Sales_Amount) FROM
Sales ORDER BY Store_ID;
(c) SELECT Store_ID, SUM(Sales_Amount) FROM
Sales GROUP BY Store_ID;
(d) SELECT Store_ID, SUM(Sales_Amount) FROM
Sales HAVING UNIQUE Store_ID;

Ans. (c) SELECT Store_ID, SUM(Sales_Amount) FROM
Sales GROUP BY Store_ID;

(iii) Which SQL statement lets you to list all store name whose total sales amount is over 5000 ?
(a) SELECT Store_ID, SUM(Sales_Amount) FROM
Sales GROUP BY Store_ID HAVING
SUM(Sales_Amount) > 5000;
(b) SELECT Store_ID, SUM(Sales_Amount) FROM
Sales GROUP BY Store_ID HAVING
Sales_Amount > 5000;
(c) SELECT Store_ID, SUM(Sales_Amount) FROM
Sales WHERE SUM(Sales_Amount) > 5000
GROUP BY Store_ID;
(d) SELECT Store_ID, SUM(Sales_Amount) FROM
Sales WHERE Sales_Amount > 5000 GROUP BY
Store_ID;

Ans. (a) SELECT Store_ID, SUM(Sales_Amount) FROM
Sales GROUP BY Store_ID HAVING
SUM(Sales_Amount) > 5000;

(iv) Which SQL statement lets you find the total number of stores in the SALES table?
(a) SELECT COUNT(Store_ID) FROM Sales;
(b) SELECT COUNT(DISTINCT Store_ID) FROM
Sales;
(c) SELECT DISTINCT Store_ID FROM Sales;
(d) SELECT COUNT(Store_ID) FROM Sales GROUP
BY Store_ID;

Ans. (d) SELECT COUNT(Store_ID) FROM Sales GROUP
BY Store_ID;

(v) Which SQL statement allows you to find the total sales amount for Store_ID 25 and the total sales amount for Store_ID 45?
(a) SELECT Store_ID, SUM(Sales_Amount) FROM
Sales WHERE Store_ID IN (25, 45) GROUP BY
Store_ID;
(b) SELECT Store_ID, SUM(Sales_Amount) FROM
Sales GROUP BY Store_ID HAVING Store_ID
IN (25, 45);
(c) SELECT Store_ID, SUM(Sales_Amount) FROM
Sales WHERE Store_ID IN (25,45);
(d) SELECT Store_ID, SUM(Sales_Amount) FROM
Sales WHERE Store_ID = 25 AND Store_ID
=45 GROUP BY Store_ID;

Ans. (b) SELECT Store_ID, SUM(Sales_Amount) FROM
Sales GROUP BY Store_ID HAVING Store_ID
IN (25, 45);

PART 2
Subjective Questions

• Short Answer Type Questions

1. What are the aggregate functions in SQL?

Ans. Aggregate function is a function where the values of multiple-rows are grouped together as input on certain criteria to form a single value of more significant meaning. Some aggregate functions used in SQL are
SUM ( ), AVG( ), MIN(), etc.

2. What is the purpose of GROUP BY clause in MySQL? How is it different from ORDER BY clause? **[CBSE 2012]**

Ans. The GROUP BY clause can be used to combine all those records that have identical value in a particular field or a group of fields.

Whereas, ORDER BY clause is used to display the records either in ascending or descending order based on a particular field. For ascending order ASC is used and for descending order, DESC is used. The default order is ascending order.

3. Shanya Khanna is using a table EMPLOYEE. It has the following columns:

Admno, Name, Agg, Stream [column Agg contains Aggregate marks]

She wants to display highest Agg obtained in each Stream.

She wrote the following statement:

```
SELECT Stream, MAX(Agg) FROM EMPLOYEE;
```

But she did not get the desired result. Rewrite the above query with necessary changes to help her get the desired output. **[CBSE Outside Delhi 2014]**

Ans.
```
SELECT Stream, MAX(Agg)
FROM EMPLOYEE
GROUP BY Stream;
```

4. What is the differences between HAVING clause and WHERE clause?

Ans.

WHERE clause	HAVING clause
WHERE clause is used to filter the records from the table based on the specified condition.	HAVING clause is used to filter record from the groups based on the specified condition.
WHERE clause implements in row operation.	HAVING clause implements in column operation.
WHERE clause cannot contain aggregate function.	HAVING clause can contain aggregate function.
WHERE clause can be used with SELECT, UPDATE, DELETE statement.	HAVING clause can only be used with SELECT statement.
WHERE clause is used with single row function like UPPER, LOWER etc.	HAVING clause is used with multiple row function like SUM, COUNT etc.

5. Gopi Krishna is using a table Employee. It has the following columns :

```
Code, Name, Salary, Dept_code
```

He wants to display maximum salary department wise. He wrote the following command :

```
SELECT Deptcode, Max(Salary) FROM
Employee;
```

But he did not get the desired result.

Rewrite the above query with necessary changes to help him get the desired output. **[CBSE Delhi 2014]**

Ans.
```
SELECT Deptcode, Max(Salary)
FROM Employee
GROUP BY Deptcode;
```

6. Write a query that counts the number of doctors registering patients for each day. (If a doctor has more than one patient on a given day, he or she should be counted only once .)

Ans.
```
SELECT ord_date, COUNT (DISTINCT
doctor_code) FROM Patients
GROUP BY ord_date;
```

7. Consider the following table Employee :

Table: Employee

100	Steven	King	Sking	1987-06-17	AD_PRES	24000.00	90
101	Neena	Kochhar	Nkochhar	1987-06-18	AD_VP	17000.00	90
102	Lex	De Haan	Ldehaan	1987-06-19	AD_VP	9000.00	60
103	Alexander	Hunold	Ahunold	1987-06-20	IT_PROG	6000.00	60
104	Bruce	Ernst	Bernst	1987-06-21	IT_PROG	4800.00	60
105	David	Austin	Daustin	1987-06-22	IT_PROG	4800.00	60
106	Valli	Pataballa	Vpata-balla	1987-06-23	IT_PROG	4800.00	100

Write a query to get the total salary, maximum, minimum, average salary of employees (Job_ID wise), for Dept_ID 90 only.

Ans.
```
SELECT Job_ID, SUM(Salary), AVG(Salary),
MAX(Salary), MIN(Salary)
FROM Employee
WHERE Dept_ID = '90'
GROUP BY Job_ID;
```

8. Why is it not allowed to give String and Date type arguments for SUM () and AVG() functions?

Ans. SUM() and AVG() functions take an argument of type numeric only. So, sum and Avg are not defined the String and date data.

9. Write the query for (i) and predict the output for (ii) and (iii):

Table : Product

P_ID	ProductName	Manufacture	Price
TP01	TALCOM POWDER	LAK	40
FW05	FACE WASH	ABC	45
BS01	BATH SOAP	ABC	55
SH06	SHAMPOO	XYZ	120
FW12	FACE WASH	XYZ	95

(i) To count the product manufacture wise from the table Product.

(ii)
```
SELECT Manufacture,MAX(Price),
MIN(Price), COUNT(*)FROM Product GROUP
BY Manufacture;
```

(iii)
```
SELECT Manufacture, MAX(Price) FROM
Product;
```

Ans. (i)
```
SELECT COUNT(ProductName),Manufacture
FROM Product
GROUP BY Manufacture;
```

(ii)
```
+-----+-----+-----+-----+
| LAK |  40 |  40 |  1  |
+-----+-----+-----+-----+
| ABC |  55 |  45 |  2  |
+-----+-----+-----+-----+
| XYZ | 120 |  95 |  2  |
+-----+-----+-----+-----+
```

(iii)
```
+---------+---------+
|   XYZ   |   120   |
+---------+---------+
```

• Long Answer Type Questions

10. Write commands in SQL for (i) to (iii) and output for (iv) and (v): [CBSE Sample Paper 2020]

Table: Store

StoreId	Name	Location	City	NoOfEmp	DateOpen	SalesAmt
S101	Planet Fashion	Bandra	Mumbai	7	2015-10-16	40000
S102	Vogue	Karol Bagh	Delhi	8	2015-07-14	120000
S103	Trends	Powai	Mumbai	10	2015-06-24	30000
S104	Super Fashion	Thane	Mumbai	11	2015-02-06	45000
S105	Annabelle	South Extn.	Delhi	8	2015-04-09	60000
S106	Rage	Defence Colony	Delhi	5	2015-03-01	20000

(i) To display names of stores along with Sales Amount of those stores that are located in Mumbai.

(ii) To display the details of store in alphabetical order of name.

(iii) To display the City and the number of stores located in that City, only if number of stores is more than 2.

(iv) `SELECT MIN(DateOpen) FROM Store;`

(v) `SELECT COUNT(StoreId), NoOfEmp FROM Store GROUP BY NoOfEmp HAVING MAX(SalesAmt)<60000;`

Ans. (i) `SELECT Name,SalesAmt FROM Store WHERE City='Mumbai';`

(ii) `SELECT * FROM Store ORDER BY Name;`

(iii) `SELECT City, COUNT(*) FROM Store GROUP BY Store HAVING COUNT(*)>2;`

(iv)
```
+------------------+
|   MIN(DateOpen)  |
+------------------+
|   2015-02-06     |
+------------------+
```

(v)
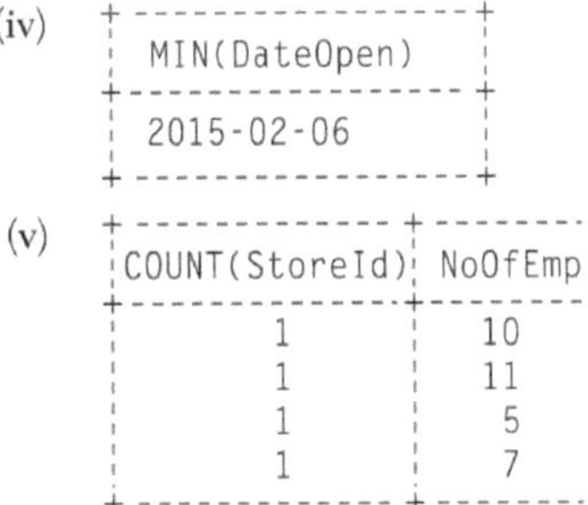
```
+----------------+----------+
| COUNT(StoreId) | NoOfEmp  |
+----------------+----------+
|       1        |    10    |
|       1        |    11    |
|       1        |     5    |
|       1        |     7    |
+----------------+----------+
```

11. Consider the table FANS:

Table: FANS

FAN_ID	FAN_NAME	FAN_CITY	FAN_DOB	FAN_MODE
F001	SUSHANT	MUMBAI	1998-10-02	MAIL
F001	RIYA	MUMBAI	1997-12-12	LETTER
F003	ANIKA	DELHI	2001-06-30	BLOG
F004	RUDRA	AJMER	2005-08-22	MAIL
F006	MIARA	KOLKATTA	1998-11-01	BLOG

Write MySQL queries for the following questions.

(i) To display the details of fans in descending order of their DOB.

(ii) To display the details of FANS who does not belong to AJMER.

(iii) To count the total number of fans of each fan mode.

(iv) To display the DOB of the youngest fan. [CBSE Sample Paper 2020]

Ans. (i) `SELECT * FROM FANS ORDER BY FAN_DOB DESC;`

(ii) `SELECT * FROM FANS WHERE FAN_CITY<>'AJMER';`

(iii) `SELECT FAN_MODE, COUNT(*) FROM FANS GROUP BY FAN_MODE;`

(iv) `SELECT MAX(FAN_DOB) FROM FANS;`

12. Consider the table DOCTOR given below. Write commands in SQL for (i) to (ii) and output for (iii) to (v).

Table : DOCTOR

ID	DOCName	Department	DOJ	Gender	Salary
1	Amit Kumar	Orthopaedics	1993-02-12	M	35000
2	Anita Hans	Paediatrics	1998-10-16	F	30000
3	Sunita Maini	Gynaecology	1991-08-23	F	40000
4	Joe Thomas	Surgery	1994-10-20	M	55000
5	Gurpreet Kaur	Paediatrics	1999-11-24	F	52000
6	Anandini Burman	Oncology	1994-03-16	F	31000
7	Siddharth Dang	Surgery	1995-09-08	M	47000
8	Rama Mukherjee	Oncology	2000-06-27	F	54500

(i) Display the names and salaries of doctors in descending order of salaries.

(ii) Display names of each department along with total salary being given to doctors of that department.

(iii) `SELECT SUM(Salary) FROM DOCTOR WHERE Department=='Surgery';`

(iv) `SELECT Department, COUNT(*) FROM DOCTOR GROUP BY Department;`

(v) `SELECT DOCName FROM DOCTOR WHERE Department LIKE '%gery%';`

Ans. (i) `SELECT DOCName, Salary FROM DOCTOR ORDER BY Salary DESC;`

(ii) `SELECT Department, SUM(Salary) FROM DOCTOR GROUP BY Department;`

(iii)
```
+-------------+
| SUM(Salary) |
+-------------+
|   102000    |
+-------------+
```

(iv)
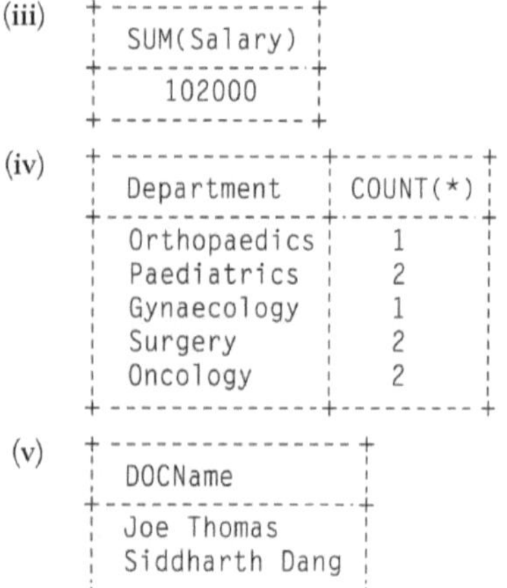
```
+-------------+----------+
| Department  | COUNT(*) |
+-------------+----------+
| Orthopaedics|    1     |
| Paediatrics |    2     |
| Gynaecology |    1     |
| Surgery     |    2     |
| Oncology    |    2     |
+-------------+----------+
```

(v)
```
+----------------+
| DOCName        |
+----------------+
| Joe Thomas     |
| Siddharth Dang |
+----------------+
```

13. Go through the following table 'Persons' and answer the questions:

Table: Persons

PId	SurName	FirstName	Gender	City	PinCode	Salary
1	Sharma	Geet	F	Udhamwara	182141	50000
2	Singh	Surinder	M	Kupwara Nagar	193222	75000
3	Jcob	Peter	M	Bhawani	185155	45000
4	Alvis	Thomas	M	Ahmed Nagar	380025	50000
5	Mohan	Garima	M	Nagar Coolangatta	390026	33000
6	Azmi	Simi	F	New Delhi	110021	40000
7	Kaur	Manpreet	F	Udhamwara	182141	42000

(i) What will be the output of the following command?

`SELECT * FROM Persons WHERE Gender ='F' AND City LIKE "%Nagar";`

(a)
```
+-----+---------+-----------+--------+---------+---------+--------+
| PId | SurName | FirstName | Gender | City    | PinCode | Salary |
+-----+---------+-----------+--------+---------+---------+--------+
| 2   | Singh   | Surinder  | M      | Kupwara | 193222  | 75000  |
|     |         |           |        | Nagar   |         |        |
+-----+---------+-----------+--------+---------+---------+--------+
| 4   | Alvis   | Thomas    | M      | Ahmed   | 380025  | 50000  |
|     |         |           |        | Nagar   |         |        |
+-----+---------+-----------+--------+---------+---------+--------+
```

(b)
```
+--------+-------------+
| Gender | City        |
+--------+-------------+
| F      | Kupwara Nagar |
| F      | Ahmed Nagar |
+--------+-------------+
```

(c)
```
+-------------------+
| City              |
+-------------------+
| Kupwara Nagar     |
| Ahmed Nagar       |
| Nagar Coolangatta |
+-------------------+
```

(d) No Output

Ans. (d) No ouput

(ii) Which column is used as primary key?

(a) PId

(b) PinCode

(c) Salary

(d) Gender

(iii) Choose the correct output.

`SELECT City, COUNT (*) FROM Persons GROUP BY City HAVING COUNT (*) > 1;`

(a)
```
+-----------+-------+
| City      | COUNT |
+-----------+-------+
| Udhamwara |   2   |
| Bhawani   |   2   |
+-----------+-------+
```

(b)
```
+-----------+-------+
| City      | COUNT |
+-----------+-------+
| Udhamwara |   2   |
+-----------+-------+
```

(c)
```
+-----------+-------+
| City      | COUNT |
+-----------+-------+
| Udhamwara |   2   |
| New Delhi |   2   |
+-----------+-------+
```

(d)
```
+-----------+-------+
| City      | COUNT |
+-----------+-------+
| New Delhi |   2   |
| Bhawani   |   2   |
+-----------+-------+
```

Ans. (i) (d) No ouput

(ii) (a) PId

(iii) (b)
```
+-----------+-------+
| City      | COUNT |
+-----------+-------+
| Udhamwara |   2   |
+-----------+-------+
```

Chapter Test

Multiple Choice Questions

1. We can use the aggregate functions in select list or the .... clause of a select statement. But they cannot be used in a .... clause.
   (a) WHERE, HAVING   (b) GROUP BY, HAVING   (c) HAVING, WHERE (d) GROUP BY, WHERE

2. If emp_id contain the set {-1, -2, 2, 3, -3, 1}, what will be the output on execution of the following MySQL statement?
```
SELECT emp id
FROM person
ORDER BY emp_id;
```
   (a) {-3, -2, -1, 1, 2, 3}   (b) {-1, 1, -2, 2, -3, 3}
   (c) {1, 2, 3, -1, -2, -3}   (d) None of the mentioned

3. Select correct SQL query from below to find the temperature in increasing order of all cites.
```
(a) SELECT city FROM weather ORDER BY temperature;
(b) SELECT city, temperature FROM weather;
(c) SELECT city, temperature FROM weather ORDER BY temperature;
(d) SELECT city, temperature FROM weather ORDER BY city;
```

4. The HAVING clause acts like a WHERE clause, but it identifies columns that meet a criterion, rather than rows.
   (a) True   (b) False
   (c) Depend on query   (d) Depend on column

5. The HAVING clause
   (a) acts exactly like WHERE clause.
   (b) acts like a WHERE clause but is used for columns rather than groups.
   (c) acts like a WHERE clause but is used for groups rather than rows.
   (d) acts like a WHERE clause but is used for rows rather than columns.

Short Answer Type Questions

6. Write a query to display the Sum, Average, Highest and Lowest marks of the students grouped by subject and sub-grouped by class.

7. Amisha wants to group the result set based on some column's value. Also, she wants that the grouped result should appear in a sorted order . In which order will she write the two clauses (for sorting and for grouping). Give example to support your answer.

8. The following query is producing an error. Identify the error and also write the correct query.
```
SELECT * FROM EMP ORDER BY NAME WHERE SALARY>=5000;
```

Long Answer Type Questions

9. Consider the following table GARMENT, write SQL commands for the statements (i) to (v).   **[CBSE Question Bank 2021]**

Table : GARMENT

GCODE	DESCRIPTION	PRICE	FCODE	READYDATE
10023	PENCIL SKIRT	1150	F03	19-DEC-08
10001	FORMAL SHIRT	1250	F01	12-JAN-08
10012	INFORMAL SHIRT	1550	F02	06-JUN-08
10024	BABY TOP	750	F03	07-APR-07
10090	TULIP SKIRT	850	F02	31-MAR-07
10019	EVENING GOWN	850	F03	06-JUN-08
10009	INFORMAL PANT	1500	F02	20-OCT-08
10007	FORMAL PANT	1350	F01	09-MAR-08
10020	FROCK	850	F04	09-SEP-07
10089	SLACKS	750	F03	20-OCT-08

(i) To display GCODE and DESCRIPTION of each GARMENT in descending order of GCODE.

(ii) To display the details of all the GARMENT, which have READYDATE in between 08-DEC-07 and 16-JUN-08 (inclusive if both the dates).

(iii) To display the average PRICE of all the GARMENT, which are made up of fabric with FCODE as F03.

(iv) To display fabric wise highest and lowest price of GARMENT from GARMENT table. (Display FCODE of each GARMENT along with highest and lowest price).

(v) To display GCODE whose PRICE is more than 1000.

10. Consider the following table SALE, write SQL commands for the statements (i) to (iv). [NCERT]

Table: SALE

InvoiceNo	CarId	CustId	SaleDate	PaymentMode	EmpID	SalePrice	Commission
I00001	D001	C0001	2019-01-24	Credit Card	E004	613247.00	73589.64
I00002	S001	C0002	2018-12-12	Online	E001	590321.00	70838.52
I00003	S002	C0004	2019-01-25	Cheque	E010	604000.00	72480.00
I00004	D002	C0001	2018-10-15	Bank Finance	E007	659982.00	79197.84
I00005	E001	C0003	2018-12-20	Credit Card	E002	369310.00	44317.20
I00006	S002	C0002	2019-01-30	Bank Finance	E007	620214.00	74425.68

(i) Display the number of cars purchased by each customer from the SALE table.

(ii) Display the customer Id and number of cars purchased if the customer purchased more than 1 car from SALE table.

(iii) Display the number of people in each category of payment mode from the table SALE.

(iv) Display the PaymentMode and number of payments made using that mode more than once.

Answers

Multiple Choice Questions

1. (b)   2. (a)   3. (c)   4. (b)   5. (c)

For Detailed Solutions

Scan the code

CHAPTER 03

Computer Networks

In this Chapter...

- Benefits of Network
- Types of Network
- Network Devices
- Network Topology

A **computer network** is a collection of computers and other hardware interconnected by communication channels that allows sharing of resources and information. A computer networking is the practice for enchancing information between two or more computer devices together for the purpose of data sharing.

These purpose of having computer network is to send and receive data stored in other devices over the network. These devices are often referred as nodes.

Benefits of Network

Computer network is very useful in modern environment. Some of the benefits of network are discussed below

(i) **File Sharing** Networking of computer helps the user to share data files.

(ii) **Software and Hardware Sharing** We can install the applications on the main server, therefore the user can access the applications centrally.

So, we do not need to install the software on every machine. Similarly, hardware can also be shared.

(iii) **Application Sharing** Applications can be shared over the network and this allows implementation of client/server applications.

(iv) **User Communication** This allows users to communicate using E-mail, newsgroups, video conferencing within the network.

(v) **Access to Remote Database** This allows users to access remote database, e.g. airline reservation database may be accessed for ticket booking.

Types of Network

Based on the size and the coverage area, networks are categorised into the following types

Local Area Network (LAN)

In a LAN, a group of computers and other devices are connected over a relatively short distance. Generally, it is a privately owned networks within a single building or campus, upto a few kilometres in size.

Users can share expensive devices, such as laser printers, as well as data on LAN and can also use the LAN to communicate with each other, by sending mails or engaging in chat sessions.

Mostly, cables are used to connect the computers in LANs. However, there is also a limit on the number of computers that can be attached to a single LAN. Now-a-days, we also have WLAN(Wireless LAN) which is based on wireless network.

Metropolitan Area Network (MAN)

This is basically a bigger version of LAN and normally uses similar technology. It might cover few buildings in a city and might either be private or public.

This is a network which spans a physical area (in the range of 5 km to 50 km) that is larger than a LAN but smaller than a WAN. MANs are usually characterised by very high-speed connections using optical fibers or other digital media and provides uplink services to Wide Area Networks (WANs) and the Internet. e.g. in a city, a MAN, which can support both data and voice might even be related to local cable television network. It is also frequently used to provide a shared connection to other networks using a link to a WAN.

Wide Area Network (WAN)

WAN spans a large geographical area, often a country or a continent and uses various commercial and private communication lines to connect computers. Typically, a WAN combines multiple LANs that are geographically separated.

Like the LAN, most WANs are not owned by any one organisation, but rather exist under collective or distributed ownership and management. The world's most popular WAN is the Internet.

Personal Area Network (PAN)

PAN refers to a small network of communication. It is a computer network organised around an individual person. These networks typically involve a mobile computer, a cell phone and/or a handheld computing devices such as a PDA. Person can use these networks to transfer files including E-mail and calendar appointments, digital photos and music.

These are used in a limited range, which is in the reachability of individual person. It generally covers a range of less than 10 metres and can be constructed with cables or wirelessly. Few examples of PAN are Bluetooth, Wireless USB, Z-Wave and Zigbee.

Virtual Private Network (VPN)

VPN is an encrypted connection over the Internet from a device to a network. It can be used to access region - restricted websites, shield your browsing activity from prying eyes on public Wi-Fi and more.

It prevents unauthorised people from eavesdropping on the traffic and allows the user to conduct work remotely. VPN technology is widely used in corporate environments.

Network Devices

Hardware device that are used to connect computers, printers, fax machines and other electronic devices to a network are called network device. There are many types of network devices used in networking and some of them are described below:

Repeater

It is a hardware device, which is used to amplify the signals when they are transported over a long distance. The basic function of a repeater is to amplify the incoming signal and retransmit it, to the other device. Repeaters are mainly used for extending the range. If you want to connect two computers, which are more than 100 metres apart you need repeater.

Hub

A hub is a device, used with computer systems to connect several computers together. It acts as a centralised connection to several computers with the central node or server. It is a multi-port device, which provides access to computers.

All incoming data packets received by the hub are sent to all hub ports and from them the data is sent to all the computers connected in a hub network.

There are two types of hub, which are as follows

   (i) **Active Hub** It acts as repeaters. It amplifies the signal as it moves from one device to another.

   (ii) **Passive Hub** It simply passes the signal from one connected device to another.

Switch

A switch is a hardware device, which is used to connect devices or segments of the network into smaller subsets of LAN segments.

The main purpose of segmenting is to prevent the traffic overloading in a network. Switch forwards a data packet to a specific route by establishing a temporary connection between the source and the destination. After the transmission or once the conversation is done, the connection is terminated.

There is a vast difference between switch and hub. A hub forward each incoming packet (data) to all the hub ports, while a switch forwards each incoming packet to the specified recipient.

Gateway

A gateway is a device, which is used to connect dissimilar networks. The gateway establishes an intelligent connection between a local network and external networks, which are completely different in structure.

The gateway is a node in a network, which serves as a proxy server and a firewall system and prevents the unauthorised access. It holds the information from a website temporarily, so that the repeated access to same website or web page could be directed to the proxy server instead of actual web server. Thus, it helps in reducing the traffic load.

Bridge

It serves a similar function as switches. A bridge filters data traffic at a network boundary. Bridges reduce the amount of traffic on a LAN by dividing it into two segments. Traditional bridges support one network boundary, whereas switches usually offer four or more hardware ports. Switches are sometimes called multi-port bridges.

Router

A router is used to connect different networks together. i.e. for two or more LANs to be interconnected, you need a router.

It is a hardware device, which is designed to take incoming packets, analyse the packets, moving and converting the packets to another network interface, dropping the packets, directing packets to the appropriate locations, etc.

MODEM (MOdulator-DEModulator)

It is a device that converts digital signal to analog signal (modulator) at the sender's site and converts back analog signal to digital signal (demodulator) at the receiver's end, in order to make communication possible *via* telephone lines. It enables a computer to transmit data over telephone or cable lines.

There are two types of MODEM, which are as follows

  (i) **Internal Modem** Fixed within a computer.

  (ii) **External Modem** Connected externally to a computer.

When a network contains largest number of system/computer it needed modem.

Network Topology

The arrangement of computers and other peripherals in a network is called its topology.

In a computer network, there are some types of physical topology, they are

Bus Topology (Linear Topology)

A bus topology is an arrangement in which the computers and the peripheral devices are connected to a common single data line.

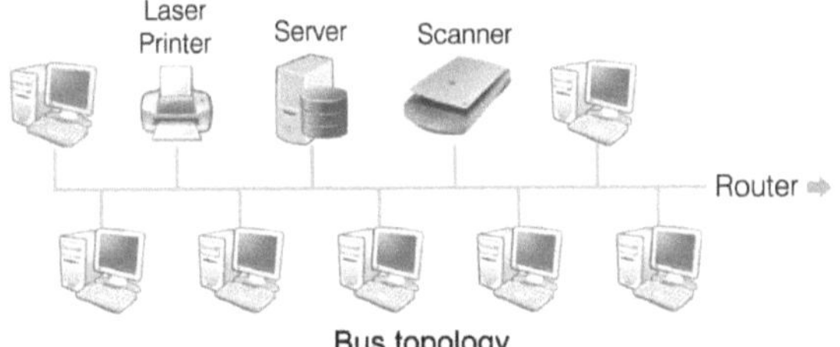

Bus topology

All the computers or devices are directly connected to the data line. The data is transmitted in small blocks known as packets. Each packet has a header containing the destination address.

When data is transmitted on the cable, the destination node identifies the address on the packet and thereby processes the data.

There are various advantages of bus topology are as follows:

- All the nodes are connected directly, so very short cable length is required.
- The architecture is very simple, reliable and linear.
- Bus topology can be extended easily on either sides.

There are various disadvantages of bus topology are as follows:

- In case of any fault occurred in data transmission, fault isolation is very difficult. We have to check the entire network to find the fault.
- Becomes slow with increase in number of nodes.
- Only a single message can travel at a particular time.

Star Topology

In star topology, each communicating device is connected to a central node which is a networking device like a hub or a switch.

The central node can be either a broadcasting device means data will be transmitted to all the nodes in the network or a unicast device means the node can identify the destination and forward data to that node only.

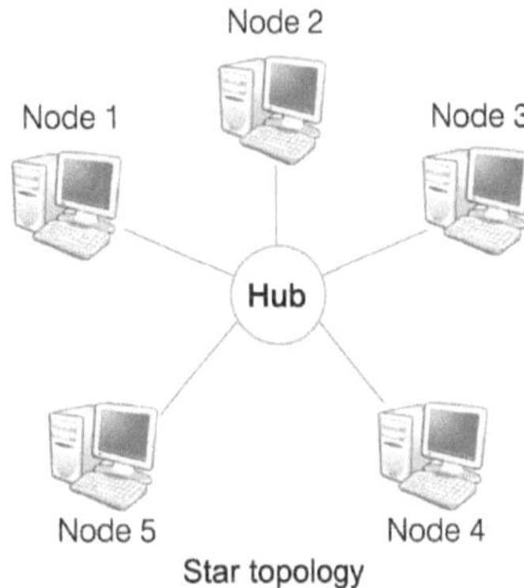

Star topology

There are various advantages of star topology are as follows:

- Installation of star topology is very easy as all the nodes are directly connected to the central node or server.
- Easy to detect faults and remove it.
- Failure of single system will not bring down the entire network.
- Allows several types of cables in same network.

There are various disadvantages of star topology are as follows:

- Requires more cable length than bus topology.
- If hub or server fails, the entire network will be disabled.
- Difficult to expand, as the new node has to connect all the way to central node.

Tree Topology

A tree topology is an extension and variation of bus topology. Its basic structure is like an inverted tree, where the root acts as a server. In tree topology, the nodes are interlinked in the form of tree.

If one node fails, then the node following that node gets detached from the main tree topology.

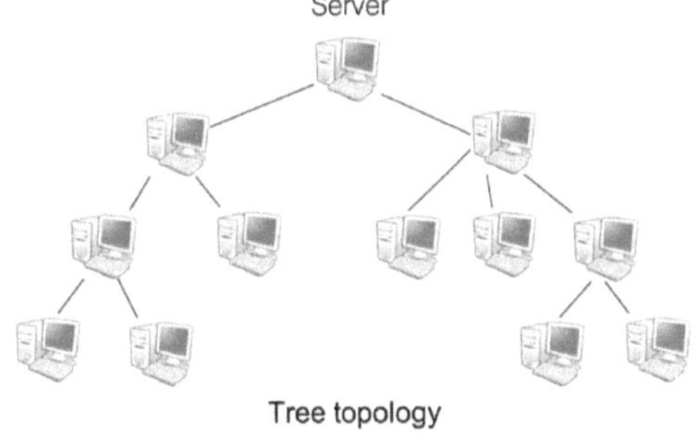

Tree topology

There are various advantages of tree topology are as follows :

- The tree topology simulates hierarchical flow of data. So, it is suitable for applications, where hierarchical flow of data and control is required.
- We can easily extend the network.
- Faulty nodes can easily be isolated from the rest of the network.

There are various disadvantages of tree topology are as follows :

- Long cables are required.
- There are dependencies on the root node.
- Installation and reconfiguration are very difficult.

Mesh Topology

It is also known as completely interconnected topology. In mesh topology, every node has a dedicated point-to-point link to every other node.

This topology is also more secure as compared to other topologies because each cable between two nodes carries different data.

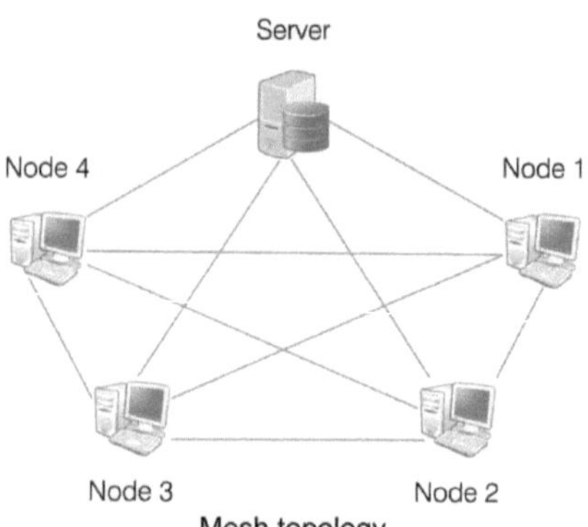

Mesh topology

There are various advantages of mesh topology are as follows:

- Excellent for long distance networking.
- Communication possible through the alternate e-Route, if one path is busy.
- A network can handle large amount of traffic since multiple nodes can transmit data simultaneously.

There are various disadvantage of mesh topology are as follows:

- Long wire/cable length is required.
- Wiring is complex and cabling cost is high in creating such networks.

Chapter Practice

Objective Questions

• Multiple Choice Questions

1. Which of the following is a collection of independent computers and other hardware interconnected by communication channels?
(a) Computer
(b) Networking
(c) Sharing
(d) None of the above

Ans. (b) A computer networking is the practice for exchanging information between two or more computer devices together for the purpose of data sharing.

2. Which of the following is an advantage of networking?
(a) Application sharing
(b) File sharing
(c) User communication
(d) All of these

Ans. (d) Computers connected in a network are able to share applications, files, resources etc. They also can communicate with each other.

3. Network formed between computers which are spread across the continents is called
(a) LAN
(b) WAN
(c) MAN
(d) WLAN

Ans. (b) Network formed between computers which are spread across the continents is called WAN. A WAN combines multiple LANS that are geographically separated.

4. Which of the following refers to a small, single site network?
(a) DSL
(b) RAM
(c) WAN
(d) PAN

Ans. (d) PAN refers to a small network of communication. It is a computer network organised around an individual person. These networks typically involve a mobile computer, a cell phone and/or a handheld computing devices such as a PDA.

5. Modulation and demodulation is performed by
(a) microwave
(b) satellite
(c) modem
(d) gateway

Ans. (c) It is a device that converts digital signal to analog signal (modulator) at the sender's site and converts back analog signal to digital signal (demodulator) at the receiver's end.

6. A modem is connected in between a telephone line and a
(a) computer
(b) serial port
(c) network
(d) communication adapter

Ans. (a) Modems has to be connected internally or externally with a computer.

7. Geometric arrangement of devices on the network is called
(a) topology
(b) protocols
(c) media
(d) LAN

Ans. (a) Geometric arrangement of devices on the network is called topology. It is the arrangement of how computers will be connected with each other.

8. In which of the topology, network components are connected to the same cable?
(a) Star
(b) Ring
(c) Bus
(d) Mesh

Ans. (c) In bus topology, network components are connected to the same cable. The figure explains the arrangement:

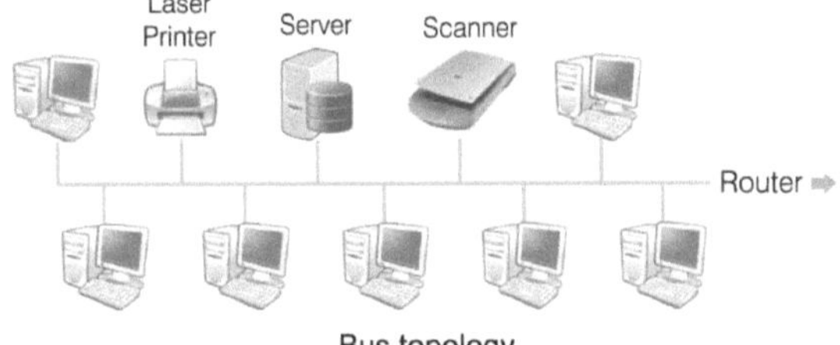

9. Which is the name of the network topology in which there are bi-directional links between each possible node?
(a) Ring
(b) Mesh
(c) Tree
(d) None of these

Ans. (b) In mesh topology, every node has a dedicated point-to-point link to every other node, that is why bi-directional links are possible.

10. Suggest the most suitable type of network topology he should use in order to maximise speed and make each computer independent of network breakdowns.   **[CBSE Question Bank 2021]**
(a) Bus topology   (b) Star topology
(c) Ring topology   (d) Mesh topology

Ans. (b) Start Topology allows several types of cables in same network, which increases speed. Failure of single system will not bring down the entire network and all system are connected to the central hub.

11. In order to allow data transfer from server to only the intended computers which network device is required in the lab to connect the computers?
                [CBSE Question Bank 2021]
(a) Switch   (b) Hub
(c) Router   (d) Gateway

Ans. (a) Switch forwards a data packet to a specific route by establishing a temporary connection between the source and the destination.

12. .... network device is known as an intelligent hub.   **[CBSE Question Bank 2021]**
(a) Switch   (b) Hub
(c) Router   (d) Gateway

Ans. (a) A hub forward each incoming packet (data) to all the hub ports, while a switch forwards each incoming packet to the specified recipient.

13. Which of the following topology contains a backbone cable running through the whole length of the network?
(a) Star   (b) Bus
(c) Mesh   (d) Tree

Ans. (b) A bus topology is an arrangement in which the computers and the peripheral devices are connected to a common single data line.

14. Computer connected to a star topology fails, the entire network will
(a) also fail
(b) work unaffectedly
(c) only server will work
(d) None of the above

Ans. (b) In star topology, each communicating device is connected to a central node which is a networking device like a hub or a switch. So, when the hub fails the whole network goes down.

But when any computer in the star topology fails, the other computers in the network continue to work unaffectedly.

15. Network device that sends the data over optimising paths through connected loop is
(a) gateway   (b) hub
(c) router   (d) bridge

Ans. (c) Network device that sends the data over optimising paths through connected loop is router.

16. In specific, if systems use separate protocols, which one of the following devices is used to link two systems?
(a) Repeater   (b) Gateway
(c) Bridge   (d) Hub

Ans. (b) If the system used separate protocols, gateway device is used to link two systems.

17. If all devices are connected to a central hub, then topology is called
(a) bus topology   (b) ring topology
(c) star topology   (d) tree topology

Ans. (c) If all devices are connected to a central hub, then topology is called star topology.

• Case Based MCQs

18. Beauty lines fashion incorporation is a fashion company with design unit and market unit at Bangalore 135m away from each other. The company recently connected their LANs using Ethernet cable to share the stock related information. But after joining their LAN's they are not able to show the information due to loss of signal in between.

(i) Which device out of the following should you suggest to be installed for a smooth communication?
(a) Modem   (b) Repeater
(c) UPS   (d) None of these

(ii) Which network is suitable to connect computers across different cities?
(a) WAN   (b) MAN
(c) PAN   (d) LAN

(iii) The company wants to increase their bandwidth and speed for communication at any cost. Which of the following cable(s) is/are suitable for that?
(a) Coaxial Cable   (b) Optical Fibre
(c) Both (a) and (b)   (d) None of these

(iv) What will be the best possible connectivity out of the following? You will suggest to connect the new set up of offices in Bangalore with its London based office.
(a) Satellite Link   (b) Infrared
(c) Ethernet   (d) None of these

(v) Which of the following device will be suggested by you to connect each computer in each of the buildings?
(a) Switch   (b) Modem
(c) Gateway   (d) None of these

Ans. (i) (b) They should use repeater. As repeater is a device used to amplify the signals.

(ii) (b) **MAN** It is a computer network that connects computers within a metropolitan area, which could be a single large city, multiple cities and towns.

(iii) (*b*) **Optical Fibre** They are designed for long-distance, high-performance data networking and telecommunications. Compared to wired cables, fiber optic cables provide higher bandwidth and transmit data over longer distances.

(iv) (*a*) **Satellite Link** Through satellites communication across countries is easily possible.

(v) (*a*) Switch is a networking hardware that connects devices on a computer network to receive and forward data to the destination device. Therefore, switch will help in communication between each of the buildings.

PART 2
Subjective Questions

• Short Answer Type Questions

1. Write down any two points of differences between LAN, MAN and WAN.   **[NCERT]**

Ans. Two major points of differences among LAN, MAN and WAN are as follows:

Basics	LAN	MAN	WAN
Geographical Area	Generally within a building	Within a city	Across the continents
Distance	Upto 5 km	Upto 160 km	Unlimited

2. Which device is used to connect dissimilar networks?

Ans. A gateway is a device, which is used to connect dissimilar networks. The gateway establishes an intelligent connection between a local network and external network, which are completely different in structure. Gateway also serve as proxy server and a firewall system that prevents the unauthorised access.

3. Identify the following devices:

(i) An intelligent device that connects several nodes to form a network and redirects the received information only to intended node(s).

(ii) A device that regenerates (amplifies) the received signal and re-transmits it to its destinations.

(iii) A device that is used to connect different types of networks. It performs the necessary translation so that the connected networks can communicate properly.

(iv) A device that converts data from digital bit stream into an analog signal and *vice-versa*.
    [Delhi 2014]

Ans. (i) Switch   (ii) Repeater

     (iii) Router   (iv) Modem

4. Write one advantage of bus topology of network. Also, illustrate how four computers can be connected with each other using star topology of network?

Ans. **Advantage of Bus Topology** In bus topology, computers can be connected with each other using server (host) along a single length of cable.

Four computers can be connected with each other using star topology in the following way:

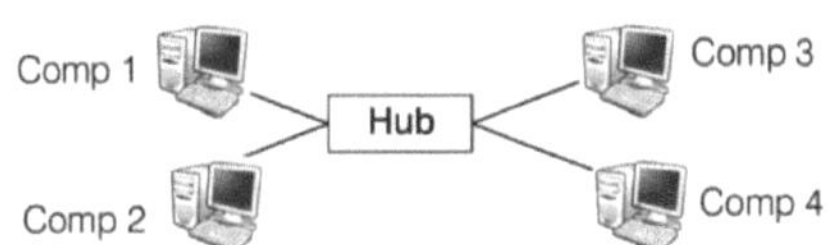

5. In networking, what is WAN? How is it different from LAN?

Ans. The network which connects the different countries is known as WAN.

Differences between LAN and WAN are as follows:

LAN	WAN
LAN stands for Local Area Network.	WAN stands for Wide Area Network.
The speed of LAN is high.	The speed of WAN is slower than LAN.
There is less congestion in LAN.	There is more congestion in WAN.
There is more fault tolerance in LAN.	There is less fault tolerance in WAN.
LAN's design and maintenance is easy.	WAN's design and maintenance is difficult than LAN.
LAN covers small area, i.e. within the building.	WAN covers large geographical area.
Transmission medium used in LAN is co-axial or UTP cable.	WAN uses satellite link as a transmission or communication medium.

6. Define hub and write its functions and types.

Ans. A hub connects several computers together and acts as a central node or server.

Functions of a Hub

- Interconnects number of computers or users.
- All the incoming data packets received by the hub are send to all hub ports and from their, the data is sent to all the computers, connected in a hub network.

Hub are of two types

(i) **Active Hub** It acts as repeater. It amplifies the signal as these move from one device to another.

(ii) **Passive Hub** It simply passes the signal from one connected device to another.

7. Mr. Kavye Shastri, General Manager of Unit Nations corporate recently discovered that the communication between his company's accounts office and HR office is extremely slow and signals drop quite frequently. These offices are 120 m away from each other and connected by an ethernet cable.

(i) Suggest him a device which can be installed in between the offices for smooth communication.

(ii) What type of network is formed by having this kind of connectivity out of LAN, MAN and WAN? **[Delhi 2012]**

Ans. (i) The device that can be installed between the office for smooth communication is repeater.

(ii) The type of network is Local Area Network (LAN).

8. Define repeaters with its two types.

Ans. Repeaters are used to amplify the signals, when they are transported over a long distance.

Repeaters are of two types

(i) **Amplifier** It amplifies or boosts the incoming signals. So, it amplifies both the signal and any concurrent noise.

(ii) **Signal Repeater** It only amplifies the signal and filters out the noise signals. So, we get only the clear signal at the receiver end.

9. When the computer network uses telephone lines as communication channel then MODEM is used as a data communication device. Now, explain the working of MODEM.

Ans. Modem performs the task of modulation at sender's site and Demodulation at the receiver's site. Basically, our computer generates data in the form of digital signals, which need to be forwarded to the receiver through telephone lines. Since, telephone lines can carry only analog signals. So, digital signals need to be converted to analog signals at sender's site, this is called modulation.

10. Write one advantage of star topology over bus topology and one advantage of bus topology over star topology.

Ans. **Advantage of star topology over bus topology** The star topology is the most reliable as there is a direct connection of every nodes in the network with the central node, so any problem in any node will affect the particular node only. While in bus topology, if problem exists in common medium, it will affect the entire node.

Advantage of bus topology over star topology Extension of network is very easy in bus topology. We can connect new node along its length. While in star topology, it is difficult to expand, as the new node has to connect all the way to central node and there is not available port in central node.

11. When would you prefer

(i) hubs over repeaters,

(ii) bridges over hubs and

(iii) switch over other network devices?

Ans. (i) We would prefer hubs over repeaters when the distance are short.

(ii) We would prefer bridges over hubs when we need to connect multiple networks.

(iii) We would prefer switch over other network devices when we want to segment networks into different sub-networks to prevent traffic overloading.

12. Define the following terms:

(i) Baud

(ii) Hubs

(iii) Repeaters

Ans. (i) **Baud** Baud is a unit of measurement for the information-carrying capacity of a communication channel.

(ii) **Hubs** In computer networking, a hub is a small, simple, low-cost device that joins multiple computers together.

(iii) **Repeaters** It is a device that amplifies and restores the signal before it gets degraded and transmits the original signal back to the destination. A repeater is a re-generator and not an amplifier.

13. Write a short note on mesh topology.

Ans. In a mesh topology, every device is connected to another device *via* a particular channel.

Every device is connected with another *via* dedicated channels. These channels are known as links.

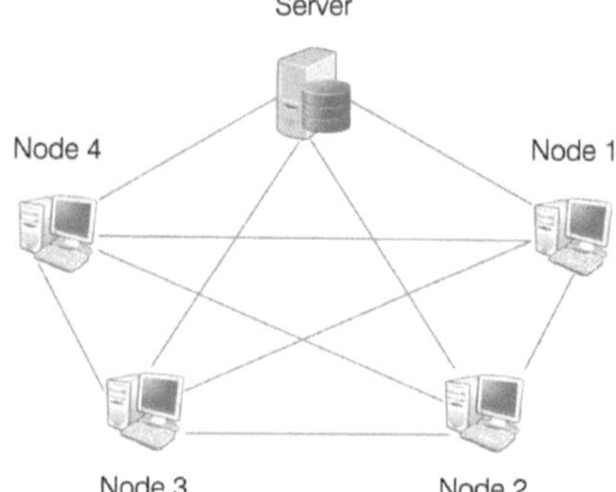

Advantages of mesh Topology

- It is robust.
- The fault is diagnosed easily. Data is reliable because data is transferred among the devices through dedicated channels or links.
- Provides security and privacy.

Disadvantages of mesh Topology

- Installation and configuration are difficult.
- The cost of cables is high as bulk wiring is required, hence suitable for less number of devices.
- The cost of maintenance is high.

• Long Answer Type Questions

14. Eduminds University of India is starting its first campus in a small town Parampur of central India with its centre admission office in Delhi. The university has three major buildings comprising of Admin Building, Academic Building and Research Building in the 5 km area campus. As a network expert, you need to suggest the network plan as per (i) to (iii) to the authorities keeping in mind the distances and other given parameters.

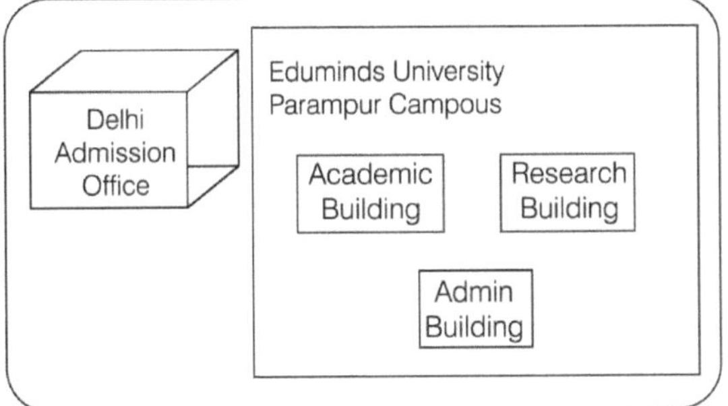

Expected wire distances between various locations:

Research Building to Admin Building	90 m
Research Building to Academic Building	80 m
Academic Building to Admin Building	15 m
Delhi Admission office to Parampur Campus	1450 km

Expected number of computers to be installed at various locations in the university are as follows:

Research Building	20
Academic Building	150
Admin Building	35
Delhi Admission Office	5

(i) Suggest the authorities, the cable layout amongst various buildings inside the university campus for connecting the building.

(ii) Suggest the most suitable place (i.e. building) to house the server of this organisation, with a suitable reason.

(iii) Suggest an efficient device from the following to be installed in each of the buildings to connect all computers.

(a) Gateway

(b) Modem

(c) Switch

Ans. (i) The suggested cable layout is as follows :

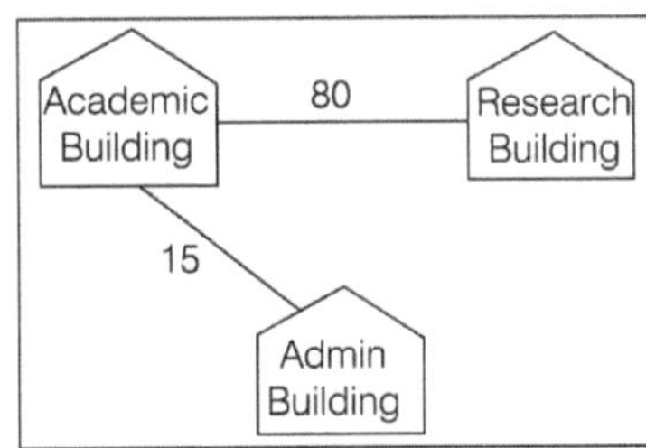

(ii) The most suitable place (i.e. block) to house the server of this university is Academic Block, because there are maximum number of computers in this block and according to 80-20 rule 80% of traffic in a network should be local.

(iii) (c)The efficient device to be installed in each of the blocks to connect all the computers is switch.

15. Bias Methodologies is planning to expand their network in India starting with three cities in India to build infrastructure for research and development of their chemical products. The company has planned to setup their main office in Pondicherry at three different locations and have named their offices as Back Office, Research Lab and Development Unit.

The company has one more research office namely Corporate Unit in Mumbai. A rough layout of the same is as follows:

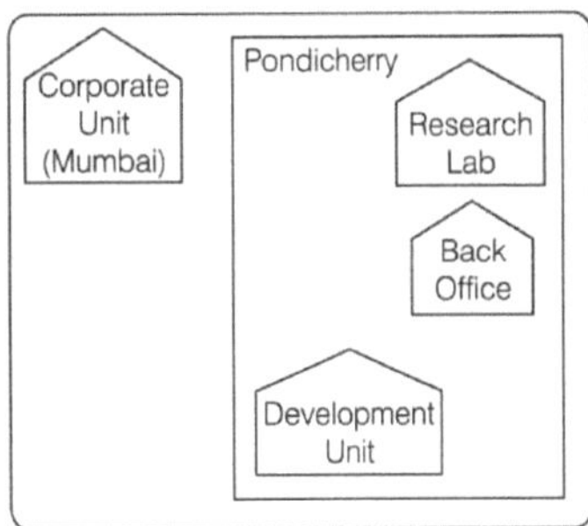

Approximate distance between these offices is as follows:

From	To	Distance
Research Lab	Back Office	110 m
Research Lab	Development Unit	16 m
Research Lab	Corporate Unit	1800 m
Back Office	Development Unit	13 m

In continuation of the above, the company experts have planned to install the following number of computers in each of these offices.

To	Distance
Research Lab	158
Development Unit	90
Back Office	79
Corporate Unit	51

(i) Suggest the kind of network required (out of LAN, MAN, WAN) for connection each of the following office unit.

(a) Research Lab and Back Office

(b) Research Lab and Development Unit

(ii) Which of the following devices will you suggest for connecting all the computers with each of their office units?

(a) Switch/Hub

(b) Modem

(c) Telephone

(iii) Suggest a cable/wiring layout for connecting the company's local office units located in Pondicherry. Also, suggest an effective method/technology for connecting the company's office located in Mumbai. **[Delhi 2008]**

Ans. (i) (a) The type of network between the Research Lab and the Back Office is LAN (Local Area Network).

(b) The type of network between Research Lab and Development Unit is MAN (Metropolitan Area Network).

(ii) (a) The suitable device for connecting all the computers within each of their office units is switch/hub.

(iii) The cable/wiring layout for connection is as follows:

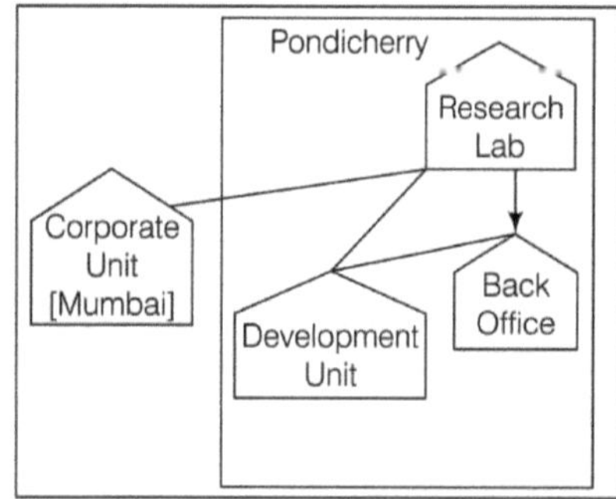

16. China Middleton Fashion is planning to expand their network in India, starting with two cities to provide infrastructure for distribution of their products.

The company has planned to setup their main office in Chennai at three different locations and have named their offices as Production Unit, Finance Unit and Media Unit. The company has its Corporate Unit in Delhi.

A rough layout of the same is as follows:

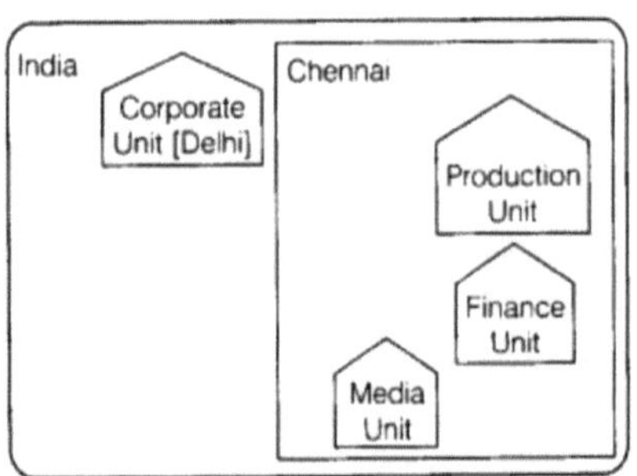

Approximate distance between these units is as follows:

From	To	Distance
Production Unit	Finance Unit	70 m
Production Unit	Media Unit	15 m
Production Unit	Corporate Unit	2112 m
Finance Unit	Media Unit	15 m

In continuation of the above, the company experts have planned to install the following number of computers in each of these units.

To	Distance
Production Unit	150
Finance Unit	35
Media Unit	10
Corporate Unit	30

(i) Suggest the kind of network required (out of LAN, MAN, WAN) for each of the following units.

(a) Production Unit and Media Unit

(b) Production Unit and Finance Unit

(ii) Which of the following devices will you suggest for connecting all computers with each of their office units?

(a) Switch/Hub   (b) Modem

(c) Telephone

(iii) Suggest a cable/wiring layout for connecting the company's local office units located in Chennai.

Also, suggest an effective method/technology for connecting the company's office unit located in Delhi. **[All India 2008]**

Ans. (i) (a) The type of network between the Production Unit and Media Unit is MAN (Metropolitan Area Network).

(b) The type of network between Production Unit and Finance Unit is LAN (Local Area Network).

(ii) (a) The suitable device for connecting all the computers within each of their office units is switch/hub.

(iii) The cable/wiring layout for connection is as follows:

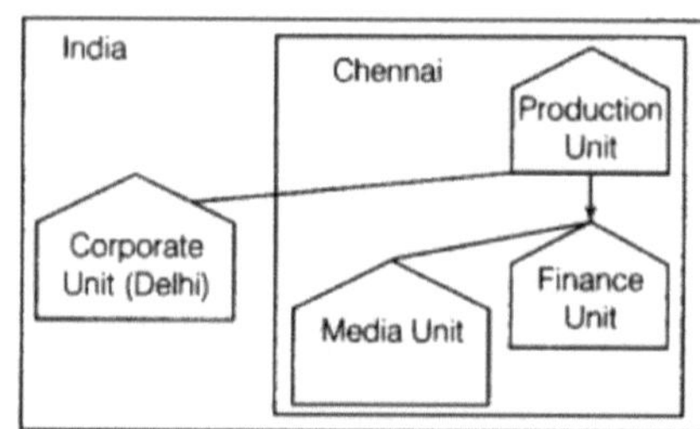

17. Bhartiya Connectivity Association is planning to spread their offices in four major cities of India to provide regional IT infrastructure support in the field of education and culture.

The company has planned to setup their head office in New Delhi in three locations and have named their New Delhi offices as Front Office, Back Office and Work Office. The company has three more regional offices as three major cities of India. A rough layout of the same is as follows:

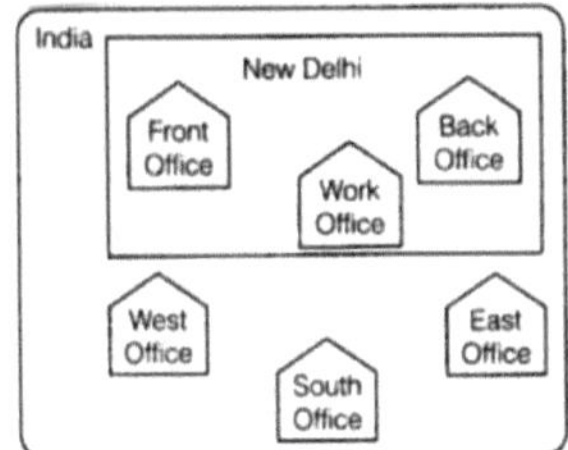

Approximate distances between these offices as per network survey team is as follows:

Place from	Place to	Distance
Back Office	Front Office	10 m
Back Office	Work Office	70 m
Back Office	East Office	1291 m
Back Office	West Office	790 m
Back Office	South Office	1952 m

In continuation of the above, the company experts have planned to install the following number of computers in each of their offices.

Back Office	100	Front Office	20
Work Office	50	East Office	50
West Office	50	South Office	50

(i) Suggest the network type (out of LAN, MAN, WAN) for connecting each of the following set of the their offices.

(a) Back Office and Work Office

(b) Back Office and South Office

(ii) Which device will you suggest to be procured by the company for connecting all the computers with each of their offices out of the following devices?

(a) Switch/Hub   (b) Modem

(c) Telephone South Office, East Office and West Office located with offices located in New Delhi

(iii) Suggest the cable/wiring layout for connecting the company's local offices located in New

Delhi. Also, suggest an effective method for connecting the company's regional offices East Office, West Office and South Office with offices located in New Delhi.

Ans. (i) (a) The type of network between the Back Office and the Work Office is LAN (Local Area Network).

(b) The type of network between the Back Office and the South Office is WAN (Wide Area Network).

(ii) (a) The suitable device for connecting all the computers in each of their offices is switch/hub.

(iii) The suggested layout for connection is as follows:

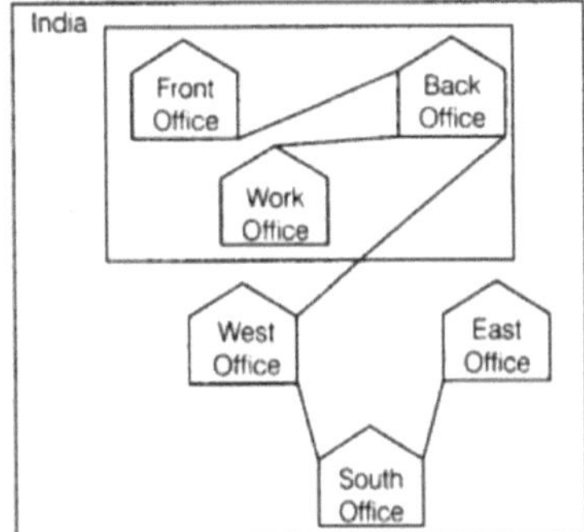

18. Hindustan Connecting World Association is planning to start their offices in four major cities in India to provide regional IT infrastructure support in the field of education and culture. The company has planned to setup their head office in New Delhi in three different locations and have named their New Delhi offices as Sales Office, Head Office and Tech Office. The company's regional offices are located at Coimbatore, Kolkata and Ahmedabad.

A rough layout of the same is as follows:

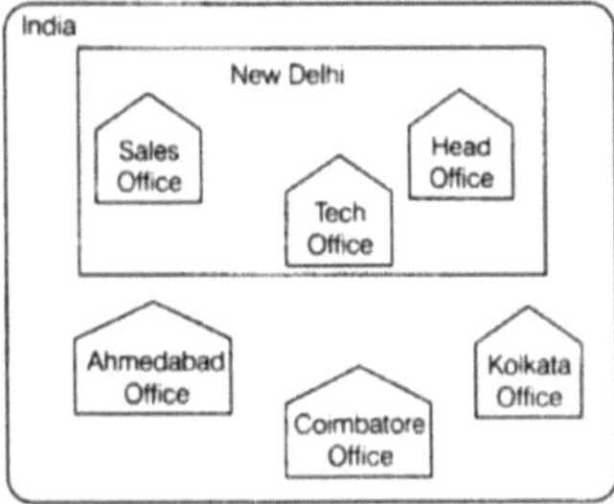

Approximate distances between these offices as per network survey team is as follows:

Place from	Place to	Distance
Head Office	Sales Office	10 m
Head Office	Tech Office	70 m
Head Office	Kolkata Office	1291 m
Head Office	Ahmedabad Office	790 m
Head Office	Coimbatore Office	1952 m

In continuation of the above, the company experts have planned to install the following number of computers in each of their offices.

Head Office	100	Sales Office	20
Tech Office	50	Kolkata Office	50
Ahmedabad Office	50	Coimbatore Office	50

(i) Suggest the network type (out of LAN, MAN, WAN) for connecting each of the following set of their offices.

(a) Head Office and Tech Office

(b) Head Office and Coimbatore Office

(ii) Which device will you suggest to be procured by the company for connecting all computers within each of their offices out of the following devices?

(a) Modem

(b) Telephone

(c) Switch/Hub

(iii) Suggest the cable/wiring layout for connecting the company's local offices located in New Delhi.

Also, suggest an effective method/technology for connecting the company's regional offices at Kolkata, Coimbatore and Ahmedabad.

Ans. (i) (a) The type of network between the Head Office and Tech Office is LAN (Local Area Network).

(b) The type of network between the Head Office and Coimbatore Office is WAN (Wide Area Network).

(ii) (c) The suitable device for connecting all the computers in each of their offices is switch/hub.

(iii) The suggested layout for connection is as follows:

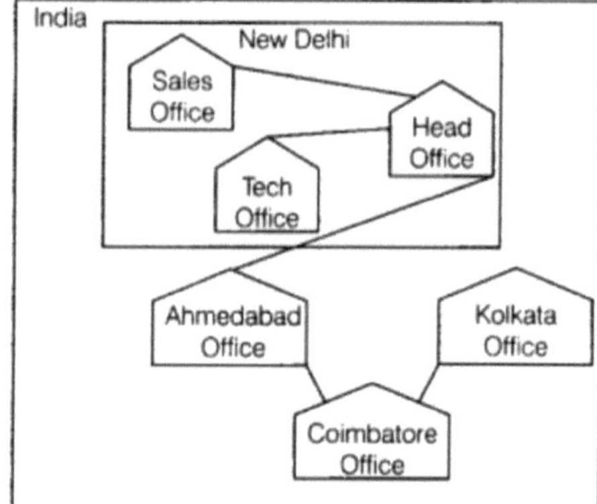

Chapter Test

Multiple Choice Questions

1. Which of the following is not a feature of networking? [CBSE 2011]

   (a) Resource sharing
   (b) Uninterrupted Power Supply (UPS)
   (c) Reduced cost
   (d) Reliability

2. What is the use of bridge in the network?

   (a) To connect LANs
   (b) To amplify signals
   (c) To control network speed
   (d) All of these

3. Data is converted in a form so as to travel over telephone lines using this device.

   (a) Modem
   (b) Hub
   (c) Switch
   (d) Router

4. If a Lawyer sharing the case files *via* bluetooth from his phone to the client's phone, considered as which of the network type?

   (a) LAN
   (b) PAN
   (c) MAN
   (d) CAN

Short Answer Type Questions

5. What is the purpose of switch in a network?

6. Give two examples of PAN and LAN type of networks. [Delhi 2016]

7. Illustrate the layout for connecting five computers in a bus and a star topology of networks. [CBSE 2015]

Long Answer Type Questions

8. Trine Tech Corporation (TTC) is a professional consultancy company. The company is planning to set up their new offices in India with its hub at Hyderabad. As a network adviser, you have to understand their requirement and suggest them the best available solutions. Their queries are mentioned as (i) to (v) below.

   Block to block distance (in metre)

Block (From)	Block (To)	Distance
Human Resource	Conference	110
Human Resource	Finance	40
Conference	Finance	80

   Expected number of computers to be in each block

Block	Computers
Human Resource	25
Finance	120
Conference	90

   (i) Which will be the most appropriate block, where TTC should plan to install their server?

   (ii) Draw a block to block cable layout to connect all the buildings in the most appropriate manner for efficient communication.

   (iii) Which of the following device will be suggested by you to connect each computer in each of the buildings?

   (a) Switch
   (b) Modem
   (c) Gateway

   (iv) The company is planning to connect its admission office in Hyderabad which is more than 1000 km from company. Which type of network will be formed?

9. Granuda consultants are setting up a secured network for their office campus at Faridabad for their day-to-day office and web based activities. They are planning to have connectivity between three buildings and the head office situated in Kolkata.

Answer the questions (i) to (iv) after going through the building positions in the campus and other details, which are given below

Distance between various buildings

Building RAVI to Building JAMUNA	120 m
Building RAVI to Building GANGA	50 m
Building GANGA to Building JAMUNA	65 m
Faridabad Campus to Head Office	1460 km

Number of Computers

Building RAVI	25
Building JAMUNA	150
Building GANGA	51
Head Office	10

(i) Suggest the most suitable place (i.e. block) to house the server of this organisation. Also, give a reason to justify your suggested location.

(ii) Suggest a cable layout of connections between the building inside the campus.

(iii) Suggest the placement of the following devices with justification:
   (a) Switch
   (b) Repeater

(iv) Consultancy is planning to connect its office in Faridabad which is more than 10 km from head office. Which type of network will be formed?

Answers

Multiple Choice Questions

   1. (b)   *2. (a)*   *3. (a)*   *4. (b)*

For Detailed Solutions

Scan the code

CHAPTER 04

Introduction to Internet and Web

In this Chapter...

- History of Internet
- Working of Internet
- World Wide Web (WWW)
- Web Server
- Website and Web Page
- Web Browser
- Electronic Mail
- Chat
- Voice over Internet Protocol (VoIP)

The term Internet is derived from the words 'interconnection' and 'networks'. A **network** is a collection of two or more computers, which are connected together to share information and resources.

The **Internet** is a worldwide system of computer networks, i.e. network of networks, it is composed of a large number of smaller interconnected networks. Through Internet, computers become able to exchange information with each other and people from all over the world can communicate with each other easily.

History of Internet

In 1969, the University of California at Los Angeles and the University of Utah were connected with the beginning of the ARPANET (Advanced Research Projects Agency NETwork) using 56 kbit/s circuits, which is sponsored by US (United States) Department of Defense (DoD). The goal of this project was to connect computers at different Universities and US defense.

In mid 80's another federal agency, the National Science Foundation (NSF) created a new high capacity network called NSFnet (National Science Foundation network), which was more capable than ARPANET.

The only drawback of NSFnet was that it allowed only academic research on its network and not any kind of private business on it.

Then, several private organisations and people started working to build their own networks, named private networks, which were later (in 1990's) connected with ARPANET and NSFnet to form the Internet. The Internet really became popular in 1990's after the development of World Wide Web (WWW).

Working of Internet

The computers on the Internet are connected to each other through small networks. These networks are connected through the gateways to the Internet backbone.

All computers on the Internet, communicate with one another using TCP/IP, which is a basic protocol of the Internet.

TCP/IP manages the transmission of data/file/document on the Internet by breaking the data/file/document into small pieces or parts called packets or datagrams. Each packet contains actual data and address part, i.e. addresses of destination and source upto 1500 characters. Functioning of TCP and IP are as follows

(i) **TCP** It breaks message into smaller packets that are transmitted over the Internet and also reassembles these smaller packets into the original message that are received from the Internet.

(ii) **IP** It handles the address part of each packet, so that the data is sent to the correct address. Each gateway on the network checks this address to see where the message is to be forwarded.

Advantages of Internet

- Greater access to information reduces research time.
- Allows you to easily communicate with other people.
- Global reach enables one to connect everyone on the Internet.
- Publishing documents on the Internet saves paper.
- A valuable resource for companies to advertise and conduct business.

Disadvantages of Internet

- Cyber frauds may take place involving credit/debit card numbers and details.
- Unsuitable and undesirable material is available that sometimes can be used by notorious people such as terrorists.
- It is a major source of computer viruses.
- Messages sent across the Internet can be easily intercepted and are open to abuse by others.
- It is difficult to check the accuracy of information available on the Internet.

Uses of Internet

Internet has been the most useful technology of the modern time, which helps us not only in our daily lives, but also in our personal and professional lives developments. Thus, some uses of Internet are as follows

- E-Commerce (Auction, buying and selling products etc.)
- Research (Online journals, magazines, information etc.)
- Education (E-learning, distance learning etc.)
- E-Governance (Online filling of application, Income Tax, Sales Tax etc.)
- E-Reservation (Online reservation, online ticket booking etc.)
- Online Payments (Credit/debit card payments etc.)
- Video Conferencing
- Exchange of Views (Files, music, folders etc.)
- Social Networking Sites (Facebook, twitter etc.)
- Entertainment (Play music, videos, games etc.)

World Wide Web (WWW)

WWW was introduced on 13th March, 1989 by Tim Berners Lee. It is often abbreviated as the web or WWW or W3. WWW is a wide area network of Internet that supports different web protocols.

World Wide Web is a common example of information protocol/service that can be used to send and receive information over the Internet (between clients and servers). It supports various types of application such as

(i) **Multimedia** It includes different types of texts, movies, music, pictures, graphics, sounds, animations, etc.

(ii) **HyperText** It includes the links of different types of information resources.

(iii) **Graphical User Interface (GUI)** It is a type of interface that allows users to interact with the web through graphical icons, buttons, labels, etc. At the time of using GUI, the user does not need to type any text command.

World Wide Web is based on client/server software design. A client/server software design requires two types of software to work in communication environment

(i) **Client Software** It is a type of software, which is used by a client (or user) to request some information from web server. e.g. Web browsers.

(ii) **Server Software** It is a type of software, which is used by the server to answer the requests and provide the required information. e.g. Microsoft, Oracle, etc.

It is possible to use your local computer as a server but usually you want to have a fixed server, which runs 24×7 hours. So, more advanced and large systems are used as a server instead of local computers.

WWW Attributes

WWW provides various attributes, which are as follows:

(i) **User-friendly** The WWW resource works smoothly with most web browsers, such as Internet Explorer, Firefox etc.

(ii) **Multimedia documents** WWW allows users to create and display web pages that contain various graphics, audio, video, animation and text.

(iii) **Interactive** WWW provides interactivity using hyperlinks and input boxes (i.e. textboxes and checkboxes).

(iv) **Frames** WWW supports frames that allow users to display more than one independent section on a single web page.

Web Address or URL

URL stands for Uniform Resource Locator. The term 'web address' is a synonym for a URL that uses the HTTP/HTTPs protocols. Each website has a unique address called URL.

e.g. the website of Microsoft has a web address or URL as http://www.microsoft.com.

URL is usually pronounced by sounding out each letter but in some quarters, pronounced 'Earl'. URL is the global address of documents and other resources on the World Wide Web.

The first part of the URL is called a **protocol identifier** and it indicates what protocol is to be used. The second part is called **resource name** and it specifies the **IP address** or the **domain name**, where the resource is located. The protocol identifier and the resource name are separated by a colon and two forward slashes.

The Internet structure of the world wide web is build on a set of rules called **HyperText Transfer Protocol** (HTTP) and a page description language called **HyperText Markup Language** (HTML).

HTTP uses Internet address in a special format called a URL. The most general form of a URL syntax is as follows:

```
protocol://domain name/<directory path>
/<object name>
```

Elements of URL

The element of this syntax are as follows:

Part	Description
Protocol	It represents the name of the protocol, which is used to transfer the data or web page.
Domain name	It represents the name of web server where the web page reside. It consists of three elements as host_name.domain_name.domain_type
Directory path	It represents the location of the web page on the web server or represents the file path on server.
Object name	It represents the name of the file with its extension to specify the file type.

e.g. `ftp://www.pcwebopedia.com/en/stuff.exe`
`http://www.pcwebopedia.com/us/index.html`

The first example specifies an executable file that should be fetched using the FTP protocol and the second example specifies a web page that should be fetched using the HTTP protocol.

Here, these URL consists of

- Protocol: ftp or http
- Host name: www
- Domain name: pcwebopedia
- Domain type: com
- File path: en or us
- File name with extension: stuff.exe or index.html

Types of URL

There are mainly two types of URL as follows

(i) **Absolute URL** It is the type of URL, which uses the complete web path of a file to provide the location of the resource, i.e. they provide the actual domain name. e.g.
`"http://www.oracle.sun.com/en/index.html"`

(ii) **Relative URL** It is the type of URL that defines the path of an URL on a domain, without including the domain name. Relative URLs are more convenient because they are short in length, more portable in website maintenance.
e.g. We specified only
`".../images/house.png"`

Web Server

A web server is a program that runs on a computer connected to the Internet.It is simply a computer with an Internet connection that runs software designed to send out HTML, DHTML, XML or Java based pages and other file formats such as multimedia files. Web server can refer to either the hardware or software, that helps to deliver web content that can be accessed through the Internet. The primary function of a web server is to deliver web pages on the request of client using the HTTP. This means delivery of HTML documents and any additional content that may be included in a document such as images, stylesheets and scripts.

Services Provided by a Server

There are different services provided by a server as follows

(i) **Centralised File Storage** The storage capacity is directly determined by the disk space that is essential to store databases, files and other media. Servers help the users to save their files or data on file server and access these data on any networked computer.

(ii) **Resource Sharing** In network, printers and scanners can be attached directly and only authorised users are able to use these shared equipments (like printers and scanners). Web server helps for resource sharing request.

(iii) **Centralised Backup** A website needs backup at regular intervals of its files and the databases. Web server helps to maintain backup and save your data from many adverse situations.

There are various types of web server, which are available for different platforms. Some of the common web servers are described below:

Apache Web Server

This server was specially developed for the UNIX platform but is presently available also for the windows and other platforms. It is an open source and free-distributed software, available from Apache software foundation.

Microsoft Internet Information Server (Microsoft IIS)

It is a protocol server. It is implemented as a set of several systems such as HTTP, FTP, NTTP. The Microsoft IIS is built into the Microsoft Windows NT Server operating system. It is capable for only running on windows platform.

Netscape Enterprise Web Server

It is a web server developed by Netscape communications corporation. The product was renamed Sun Java system web server, reflecting the product acquisition by Sun Microsystem. It is used to run the web page and give the response to client.

Web Hosting

A web hosting service is a type of Internet hosting service that allows individuals and organisations to make their website accessible *via* the World Wide Web. A web host is in the business of providing server space, web services and file maintenance for websites controlled by individuals or companies that do not have their own web servers. Many ISPs, such as America Online will allow subscribers a small amount of server space to host a personal web page. Other commercial ISPs will charge the user a fee depending on the complexity of the site being hosted.

Web hosting can be of four types as follows:
- Free Hosting
- Virtual or Shared Hosting
- Dedicated Hosting
- Co-location Hosting

Website

A group of related web pages that follow the same theme and are connected together with hyperlinks is called a website. In other terms, "A website is a collection of digital documents, primarily HTML files, that are linked together and that exist on the web under the same domain".

A website displays related information on a specific topic. Each website is accessed by its own address known as URL (Uniform Resource Locator).

e.g. `http://www.carwale.com` is a website, while `http://www.carwale.com/new/` is a web page.

Components of Website

There are various components of website as follows

(i) **Navigation** It helps users in easily navigating the complete site and it also helps the search engine to get an idea of the structure of the website.

(ii) **Web Hosting** Every website has a set of files and folder in the backend which makes the site possible to be accessible by everyone in the world and those files have to be stored somewhere for that web hostings are used.

(iii) **Content** Blogs will require different content than service or business websites but content will be needed for every website.

(iv) **Home Page** The first or main page of a website is called home page.

(v) **Address** This is the URL or address of a website.

(vi) **Web Portal** It is specially designed website that often serves as the single point of access for information. It also has hyperlinks to many other websites.

Web Page

Web page is an electronic document designed using HTML. It displays information in textual or graphical form. Traversal from one web page to another web page is possible through hyperlinks. A web page can be of two types:

Static Web Page

A web page which displays same kind of information whenever a user visits, is known as a static web page. A static web page generally has .htm or .html as extension.

e.g. A page that contains school or company information. The content of this page will not change every day unless the HTML file is manually edited by a programmer who maintains it.

Dynamic Web Page

An interactive web page is a dynamic web page. A dynamic web page uses scripting languages to display changing content on the web page. Such a page generally has .php, .asp or .jsp as extension.

e.g. When you login to your Yahoo E-mail account to check and to send E-mails. Moreover, the list of E-mail messages changes as it arrives or as the list is deleted or is moved to another folder.

Differences between Static and Dynamic Web Pages

Key	Static Web Page	Dynamic Web Page
Definition	Static web pages are generally simple HTML written pages which serve as response from browser to server in which all the information and data is static in nature and it does not get changed until someone changed it manually.	On other hand dynamic web pages are the pages written in some more complex language such as ASP.NET in which data is rendered after some interpretation and capacity to produce distinctive content for different calls.
Complexity	As mentioned in above point as data in static web pages is static and do not require any interpretation before rendering so static web pages are simple in complexity.	Dynamic web pages on other hand does the interpretation process which make data dynamic in nature and due to which dynamic web pages become complex in complexity as compare to static web pages.
Language used	Static web pages are generally written in simpler languages such as HTML, JavaScript, CSS, etc.	On other dynamic web pages are written in more complex languages such as CGI, AJAX, ASP, ASP.NET, etc.
Rendered Data	For static web pages data do not changes until someone changes it manually and hence data is static in nature.	On other hand for dynamic web page data is first interoperate at server side and due to which it does not remain same on every call and this makes data dynamic in nature.
Time	Static web pages due to static data take less time to get load.	While dynamic web pages due to dynamic data take comparatively more time as compare to static web pages.
Database	In static web pages generally no involvement of database for data redecoration.	On other hand in case of dynamic web page database is used for data redecoration.

Differences between Website and Web Page

Website	Web Page
Web site is a collection of web pages displayed on the web with a client-like browser.	It is part of website that includes information and content and is displayed on the browser to user or visitor.

Website	Web Page
It contains more than one web pages that contain information.	It is a single document display on the browser.
It is a combination of web pages created using HTML and CSS.	Information is usually written in HTML language.
It is a place used to display content.	It is content displayed on the website.
It requires more time to develop the website as compared to web pages.	It requires less time to develop a web page as compared to the website.
It includes content about several entities.	It includes content or information about a single entity.
It can be accessed using HTTP, DNS (Domain Name System) protocols.	It can be accessed through web browser.
There is no such extension included in the URL of the website.	URL of web page include extension.
It includes web pages, related content and hyperlinks.	It might include text, graphics, hyperlinks, etc.
They are used to establish credibility as business and also to increase the positive impression about the company or business that in turn increase user experience.	They are used to provide information with related pictures, videos to user.

Web Browser

A web browser (commonly referred to as a browser) is a software application for retrieving, presenting and traversing information resources on the World Wide Web. Hyperlinks present in resources enable users easily to navigate their browsers to related resources. Although, browsers are primarily intended to use the World Wide Web, they can also be used to access information provided by web servers in private networks or files in file systems. The popular web browsers are Google Chrome, Mozilla Firefox, Internet Explorer, Opera, Safari, Lynx and Netscape Navigator.

Browsers are of two types

(i) **Text-Based Web Browsers** are the web browsers that support text only, i.e. these browsers do not support graphics. e.g. Lynx.

(ii) **Graphical-Based Web Browsers** provide a Graphical User Interface (GUI) where the user can jump from one web page to another by clicking on the hyperlink on a web page. e.g. Chrome, Internet Explorer, Mozilla Firefox, etc.

Web Browser Toolbar

A major part of the user interface for a browser is the toolbar. This appears at   the top of the browser window, above the viewing pane and it can perform a number of critical functions.

Major functions of browser toolbar are as follows

(i) **Back** This takes you one step back in your history, to the page you were on before the current page.

(ii) **Forward** It allows you to move forward through your history, to where you were before you used the Back button.

(iii) **Address Bar** This is a text box that displays the URL of the current page.

(iv) **Stop** This will be found either just inside the address bar or just next to it. It only appears when the page is currently in the process of loading. If you click it, the page will stop loading.

(v) **Refresh** The Refresh or Reload button looks like a circular arrow. This button repeats the request that led to the current page, which usually cause the same page to load into the browser again.

(vi) **Bookmark** This allows you to bookmark the URL, saving it to you browser.

Electronic Mail

Electronic mail most commonly referred to as E-mail, is a method of exchanging digital messages from sender to one or more recipients. Modern E-mail operates across the Internet or other computer networks. Some early E-mail systems required that the sender and the recipient both be online at the same time, in common with instant messaging. Today's E-mail systems are based on Store-and-Forward Model. E-mail servers accept, forward, deliver and store messages. Neither the users nor their computers are required to be online simultaneously. They need to connect only briefly, typically to an E-mail server, for as long as it takes to send or receive messages. Interactions between E-mail servers and clients are governed by E-mail protocols.

E-mail Addressing

An E-mail address is composed of two separate parts.

- Your personal identity or account name (user name) on that mail server.
- The domain name of the mail server computer on which you have an E-mail account.

An E-mail address is generally of the form username@domainname.

Some examples of E-mail address are:

(i) arihant@gmail.com

(ii) webmaster@yahoo.com

In E-mail address, symbol @ is used as a separator. It separates your account name and mail server name.

Advantages of E-mail

- E-mails are easy to use. You can organise your daily correspondence, send and receive electronic messages and save them on computers.
- E-mails are fast. They are delivered at once around the world. No other form of written communication is as fast as an E-mail.

- The language used in E-mails is simple and informal.
- When you reply to an E-mail you can attach the original message so that when you answer the recipient knows, what you are talking about. This is important if you get hundreds of E-mails a day.
- It is possible to send automated E-mails with a certain text. In such a way, it is possible to tell the sender that you are on vacation. These E-mails are called auto responders.

Disadvantages of E-mail

- E-mails may carry viruses. These are small programs that harm your computer system. They can read out your E-mail address book and send themselves to a number of people around the world.
- Many people send unwanted E-mails to others. These are called spam mails. It takes a lot of time to filter out the unwanted E-mails from those that are really important.
- E-mails cannot really be used for official business documents. They may be lost and you cannot sign them.
- Your mailbox may get flooded with E-mails after a certain time so you have to empty it from time-to-time.

Difference between Cc and Bcc

Cc (Carbon copy) allows an E-mail to be send to a large number of people by writing their respective addresses separated by commas.

Bcc (Blind carbon copy) is Cc, except that the recipient does not see the list of people in the Bcc field.

Chat

Chatting is the online textual or multimedia conversation. It is widely interactive text-based communication process that takes place over the Internet. Chat with people using the Internet is somewhat similar to using the telephone for the same purpose. Chatting i.e. a virtual means of communication that involves the sending and receiving of messages, share audio and video between users located in any part of the world.

In chatting, you type a message in your chat box, which is immediately received by the recipient, then the recipient type a message in response to your message which is instantly received by you.

There are numerous chat programs that you can download, including Yahoo! messenger, windows live messenger and skype (all three of these can also do voice and video chat). In addition, there are many browser based services that do not require downloading.

e.g. Facebook has a built-in chat feature and gmail allows you to chat with your contacts whenever, you are logged into your G-mail account.

Types of Chat

Chat can be of different types. Given below are some commonly used types of chat

(i) **Instant Messaging (IM)** It is an Internet service that allows people to communicate with each other in real time through an instant messaging software. Unlike E-mails, instant messaging allows message from one person to appear right away on the other person's computer screen right after the send button is pressed. Many instant messaging services offer video calling features, Voice over Internet Protocol and web conferencing services. Web conferencing services can integrate both video calling and instant messaging abilities.

(ii) **Internet Relay Chat (IRC)** It is an application layer protocol that facilitates communication in the form of text. The chat process works on a client/server networking model. IRC clients are computer programs that users can install on their system or web based applications running either locally in the browser or on a third party server. These clients communicate with chat servers to transfer messages to other clients. IRC is mainly used for group discussion in chat rooms called "channels" although it supports private messages between two users, data transfer and various server-side and client-side commands.

(iii) **ICQ (I Seek You)** ICQ offers chatting *via* ICQ software. It is used as a conferencing tool by individuals on the Net to chat, E-mail, perform file transfers, play computer games and more.When you download ICQ program (which is free) you are assigned an ICQ number. Two or more people using ICQ can have the same nick name, but no two people can have the same ICQ number.

(iv) **Web Based Chat** It is also like IRC but it is different from it in the sense that it's on a specific website and no program is really needed to install on computer. Yahoo chat is a great example of a web based chat.

Voice over Internet Protocol (VoIP)

VoIP is a technology that enables voice communications over the Internet through the compression of voice into data packets that can be efficiently transmitted over data networks and then converted back into voice at the other end. It requires broadband connection, a computer, special phone or adaptor.

Advantages of VoIP

- The biggest single advantage of VoIP has over standard telephone systems is low cost.
- Using services such as true VoIP, subscribers can call one another at no cost to other party.
- Routing phone calls over existing data networks eliminate the need for separate voice and data networks.
- The ability to transmit more than one telephone call over a single broadband connection.

- VoIP consists advance telephone features, e.g. call routing, screen POP and IVR.

Disadvantages of VoIP

- Without power, VoIP phones are useless, so in case of emergencies during power cuts it cannot be used.
- It uses Internet protocol's packets so if packets get dropped along the way then voice quality drops.
- Even with its high quality, it cannot match the voice quality of a normal telephone line.
- It may not work for emergency service numbers like Police or Fire services.

Add-ons

Add-ons or extension are tools which integrate into your browser. They are similar to regular apps or programs, but only run when the browser runs. Add-ons can allow the viewing of certain types of web content, such as Adobe Flash Player, necessary for Netflix movies and YouTube Videos respectively.

Toolbars are another type of add-on, placing a new kind of search bar at the top of your browser window. Add-ons can work within the framework of the browser, such as changing the appearance or adding a search provider or they can provide separate functions, such as performing custom functions or adding a status bar.

How Add-ons are Installed?

There are two ways in which add-ons become installed through an external installer and through the browser's own add-on service. The add-on service is the most reliable way of installing an add-on, with the browser service providing a relative 'setting' process for the general safety of the add-on. Outside programs can also install add-ons in your browser as part of its separate installation process.

For example, Microsoft Office may place an add-on which speeds up the browser opening of office documents. These outside installers, however are also favoured by malware companies. Add-ons can be added as part of a valid program installation. These add-ons are also typically the largest consumers of resources.

How to Remove Add-ons?

Add-ons can be removed in one of two ways. Some add-ons, particularly ones installed outside of the browser, create an entry in the 'Programs' portion of the control panel. Removing these is done in the same way you uninstall any other program. Many add-ons, however can only be removed through the browser's add-on manager. In firefox, it is found by clicking the firefox button in the upper left corner and selecting Add-ons a menu items which may have a puzzle piece next to it.

Internet explorer offers the add-on manager by clicking the tools button and clicking manage add-ons.

Plug-ins

It is a piece of software that acts as an add-on to a web browser and gives the browser additional functionality. Plug-ins can allow a web browser to display additional content, it was not originally designed to display. An example of a plug-in is the free macromedia flash Player, a plug-in that allows the web browser to display animations using the flash format. As the web has become more commercial, flash has become a popular format for displaying ads in web pages.

As a result, many web users have been prompted to download the flash plug-in and have it installed on their systems. Other popular plug-ins include Quicktime Player (available on the Apple website) and Acrobat Reader (which in addition to bring a plug-in for the major browsers) is also a stand alone application used to display files using the PDF format.

How Plug-ins are Installed?

Most plug-ins are available as free downloads. To install the plug in, you visit the website of the plug-in's developer and click on a link that will download the installer for the plug-in, you have selected.

You can save the installer to an easy to find location such as the desktop or a specific folder you have created to organise all of you downloads. Once you have downloaded the installer, you can open it and follow the prompts to install the plug-in on your system. You may have to restart your web browser to enable the additional functionality provided by the plug-in.

Cookies

They are used by web developers to help users navigate their websites efficiently and perform certain functions. Due to their core role of enhancing/enabling usability or site processes, disabling cookies may prevent users from using certain websites. Cookies are created when a user's browser loads a particular website.

The website sends information to the browser, which then creates a text file. Every time the user goes back to the same website, the browser retrieves and sends this file to the website's server.

Computer cookies are created not just by the website the user is browsing but also by other websites that run ADS, widgets or other elements on the page being loaded. These cookies regulate how the ads appear or how the widgets and other elements function on the page.

Chapter Practice

Objective Questions

• Multiple Choice Questions

1. What can you do with the Internet?
   (a) Exchange information with friends and colleagues
   (b) Access pictures, sounds, video clips and other media elements
   (c) Find diverse perspective on issues from a global audience
   (d) Exchange information, access pictures, find diverse perspective on issue from a global audience

Ans. (d) Internet facility are able to exchange information, access pictures, find diverse perspective on issue from a global audience.

2. There are numerous websites, which provide search facility for searching the contents on
   (a) Internet   (b) website
   (c) web page   (d) LAN

Ans. (a) There are numerous websites, which provide search facility for searching the contents on Internet. The Internet is a huge ocean of information of resources and services such as interlinked hypertext documents of World Wide Web (WWW), online chatting, online banking, file transfer and sharing, online gathering, online education and so on and websites provide us the facility to search information from these resources.

3. The first network is
   (a) ARPANET
   (b) Internet
   (c) NSFnet
   (d) NET

Ans. (a) In 1969, the University of California at Los Angeles and the University of Utah were connected with the beginning of the ARPANET.

4. The WWW is made up of the set of interconnected .... that are linked together over the Internet.
   (a) electronic documents
   (b) web pages
   (c) files
   (d) All of the above

Ans. (b) Web pages are the HTML documents which are linked with each other and together known as website or WWW.

5. In URL, http://www.arihant.com/index.htm, which component identifies the path of a web page?
   (a) http
   (b) www.arihant.com
   (c) /index.htm
   (d) All of the above

Ans. (c) The most general form of a URL syntax is as follows
```
protocol://domain name/<directory
path>/<object name>
```
So, here we can see /<directory path>/<object name> is the path.

6. Which of the following statement(s) is/are true about URL?
   (a) URL stands for Uniform Resource Locator.
   (b) You can enter URL into address bar.
   (c) Both (a) and (b)
   (d) It is not necessary for URL to be unique.

Ans. (c) URL stands for Uniform Resource Locator. It is the global address of documents and other resources on the World Wide Web and the resources can be searched through writing resource name on the browser address bar.

7. A website is a collection of
   (a) web server   (b) web page
   (c) web browser   (d) WWW

Ans. (b) A group of related web pages that follow the same theme and are connected together with hyperlinks is called a website.

8. Home page helps viewers to find out what they can find on the particular site. Home page is the
   (a) first page of a website
   (b) index page
   (c) about page
   (d) None of the above

Ans. (a) Home page is the first page of a website.

9. Which of the following website is not used for job search?
   (a) monster.com
   (b) recruitment.com
   (c) naukri.com
   (d) Myspace

Ans. (d) Myspace is not used for searching job and rest all websites mentioned are used to search job.

10. Web page is created using language
    (a) XML   (b) Java
    (c) C   (d) HTML

Ans. (*d*) The HyperText Markup Language or HTML is the standard markup language for documents designed to be displayed in a web browser.

11. By default, web pages are saved in the .... folder.
    (a) Download   (b) Document
    (c) Picture   (d) Music

Ans. (*b*) Documents is the default location for all downloaded web pages.

12. A browser is a program, which is used to
    (a) connect to Internet
    (b) create websites
    (c) view sites on web
    (d) All of the above

Ans. (*d*) A browser is a program, which is used to connect to Internet, create websites and view sites on web. Browsers are primarily intended to use the World Wide Web, they can also be used to access information provided by web servers in private networks or files in file systems.

13. Which of the following is developed by Apple Incorporation?
    (a) Lynx   (b) Opera
    (c) Safari   (d) Mozilla Firefox

Ans. (*c*) Safari is a graphical web browser developed by Apple Incorporation, which based primarily on open-source software properties notably including WebKit. It was first introduced on Mac OS X Panther in 2003, and was later incorporated to the iPhone and iPod Touch with iPhone OS 1 in 2007.

14. Which of the following is the online textual or multimedia conversation?
    (a) VoIP
    (b) Chatting
    (c) HTML
    (d) None of the above

Ans. (*b*) Chatting, i.e. a virtual means of communication that involves the sending and receiving of messages, share audio and video between users located in any part of the world.

15. After setting up the lab and Internet in the lab, Samarth is now required to enable videos and animations to be played on the web browser for students of multimedia class. Which browser tool /service can be used for the same?
                  [CBSE Question Bank 2021]
    (a) Plug-ins
    (b) Add-ons
    (c) Control Panel
    (d) Download Settings

Ans. (*b*) Add-ons browser tool/service can be used to enable videos and animations to be played on the web browser for students of multimedia class.

16. During an international exchange programme the students need to connect to a classroom in Russia using Skype. Samarth helps the students to connect. Which type of network service is being used ?   **[CBSE Question Bank 2021]**
    (a) Instant messaging
    (b) Email messaging
    (c) VoIP
    (d) WWW

Ans. (*c*) Through VoIP Samarth can set up his classroom. VoIP is a technology that enables voice communications over the Internet through the compression of voice into data packets that can be efficiently transmitted over data networks.

• Case Based MCQs

Direction *Read the case and answer the following questions.*

17. Web server is a special computer system running on HTTP through web pages. The web page is a medium to carry data from one computer system to another. The working of the web server starts from the client or user. The client sends their request through the web browser to the web server. Web server takes this request, processes it and then sends back processed data to the client. The server gathers all of our web page information and sends it to the user, which we see on our computer system in the form of a web page. When the client sends a request for processing to the web server, a domain name and IP address are important to the web server. The domain name and IP address are used to identify the user on a large network.

  (i) Web servers are
    (a) IP addresses
    (b) computer systems
    (c) web pages of a site
    (d) a medium to carry data from one computer to another

  (ii) What does the web server need to send back information to the user?
    (a) Home address   (b) Domain name
    (c) IP address   (d) Both (b) and (c)

 (iii) What is the full form of HTTP?
    (a) HyperText Transfer Protocol
    (b) HyperText Transfer Procedure
    (c) Hyperlink Transfer Protocol
    (d) Hyperlink Transfer Procedure

  (iv) The .... translates Internet domain and host names to IP address.
    (a) domain name system
    (b) routing information protocol
    (c) Internet relay chart
    (d) network time protocol

(v) Computer that requests the resources or data from another computer is called as ………. .

(a) server   (b) client

(c) Both (a) and (b)   (d) None of these

Ans. (i) (*b*) Web servers are computer systems.

That means a web server is computer software and hardware that accepts requests *via* HTTP, the network protocol created to distribute web content or its secure variant HTTPs.

(ii) (*d*) Domain name and IP address need to send back information to the user.

(iii) (*a*) HTTP stands for HyperText Transfer Protocol. It specifies how to transfer hypertext (linked web documents) between two computers.

(iv) (*a*) Domain name system is the way the Internet domain names are stored and translated to IP addresses. The domain names systems matches the name of website to IP addresses of the website.

(v) (*b*) Computer that requests the resources or data from other computer is known as client. Client computer always make use of the software or hardware in which the service is made by the server.

PART 2
Subjective Questions

• Short Answer Type Questions

1. Define the following terms.   **[NCERT]**

(a) ARPANET

(b) ISP

(c) URL

Ans. (a) ARPANET stands for Advanced Research Projects Agency NETwork.

(b) ISP stands for Internet Service Provider

(c) URL stands for Uniform Resource Locator

2. Define home page. Give two advantages of home page.

Ans. A home page is the first page of a website. Two advantages of home page are as follows:

(i) It helps viewers to find out what they can find on that site.

(ii) Publicity of an individual or a community.

3. Give any three applications on the Internet.

          [NCERT]

Ans. Some uses of Internet are as follows:

(i) **Electronic Mail (E-mail)** The first major use of the Internet is E-mail. People used to E-mail for sharing information, data files, photos, videos, business communications and any other files instantaneously with others.

This had enabled faster communication between people and improve business efficiency.

(ii) **E-commerce** The Internet enables the selling of goods and services in online mode. There are many

E-commerce platform vendors like Amazon, Ola who aggregate several products/services available in the market and sell them through their portal to customers.

(iii) **Education** The Internet offers a wealth of educational material on any subject with structured navigation and search facilities.

One can seek any reading material and the Internet will get it for them from any server in any part of the world.

4. Sahil, a Class X student, has just started understanding the basics of Internet and web technologies. He is a bit confused in between the terms "World Wide Web" and "Internet". Help him in understanding both the terms with the help of suitable examples of each.   **[NCERT]**

Ans. **World Wide Web** is a set of programs, standards and protocols that allows the multimedia and hypertext files to be created, displayed and linked on the Internet.

e.g. www.microsoft.com, www.amazon.com, etc.

Internet is a computer-based world wide communications network, which is composed of large number of smaller interconnected networks.

e.g. Web, E-mails, Social media, etc.

While Internet is a collection of computers or networking devices connected together; WWW is a collection of documents, linked *via* special links called hyperlinks. WWW forms a large part of Internet but is not the Internet.

5. Ruhani wants to edit some privacy settings of her browser. How can she accomplish her task?

       [NCERT]

Ans. She can accomplish her task by performing following steps

Step 1 Open your web browser.

Step 2 Open browser settings.

Step 3 Look for Privacy and Security settings. If not directly found, click on Advanced settings.

Step 4 After reaching Privacy and Security settings she can edit their setting.

6. Define the structure of URL with example.

Ans.

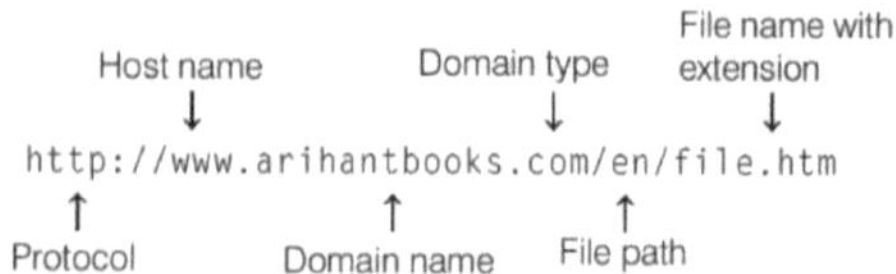

7. Mr. Lal owns a factory which manufactures automobile spare parts.

Suggest him the advantages of having a web page for his factory.

Ans. The web page provides the information to the clients about his factory of spare parts. Moreover, he can receive the order on the Internet from the clients using the web page.

8. Which page does not change until the developer modifies them?

Ans. Static pages do not change until the developer modifies them. To update a static web page, the file name must be changed manually.

9. How is an E-mail different from a chat?

Ans. In order to chat, you need have an account on the same service as the person you are chatting with. On the other hand, in case of E-mail, it is not necessary, i.e. you can have an account from any provider and you can establish your own.

10. Explain any two attributes of WWW.

Ans. Two attributes of WWW are as follows:
  (i) **User-friendly** The WWW resource works smoothly with most web browsers, such as Internet Explorer, Firefox etc.
  (ii) **Multimedia documents** WWW allows users to create and display web pages that contains various graphics, audios, videos, animation and text.

11. How many types of software are used to work in communication environment?

Ans. A client/server software design requires two types of software to work in communication environment:
  (i) **Client Software** It is a type of software, which is used by a client (or user) to request some information from web server.
  (ii) **Server Software** It is a type of software, which is used by the server to answer the requests and provide the required information.

12. Differentiate between
  (i) website and web page
  (ii) static and dynamic web pages

Ans. (i) Difference between static and dynamic web pages are as follows

Key	Static Web Page	Dynamic Web Page
Definition	Static web pages are generally simple HTML written pages which serve as response from browser to server in which all the information and data is static in nature and it does not get changed until someone changed it manually.	On other hand dynamic web pages are the pages written in some more complex language such as ASP. NET in which data is rendered after some interpretation and capacity to produce distinctive content for different calls.
Complexity	As mentioned in above point as data in static web pages is static and do not require any interpretation before rendering so static web pages are simple in complexity.	Dynamic web pages on other hand does the interpretation process which make data dynamic in nature and due to which dynamic web pages become complex in complexity as compare to static web pages.
Language used	Static web pages are generally written in simpler languages such as HTML, JavaScript, CSS, etc.	On other dynamic web pages are written in more complex, languages such as CGL, AJAX, ASP, ASP. NET, etc.
Rendered data	For static web pages data do not changes until someone changes it manually and hence data is static in nature.	On other hand for dynamic web page data is first interoperate at server side and due to which it does not remain same on every call and this makes data dynamic in nature.
Time	Static web pages due to static data take less time to get load.	While dynamic web pages due to dynamic data take comparatively more time as compare to static web pages.
Database	In static web pages, generally no involvement of database for data redecoration.	On other hand in case of dynamic web page database is used for data redecoration.

(ii) Difference between website and web page are as follows

Website	Web Page
Website is a collection of web pages displayed on the web with a client-like browser.	It is part of website that includes information and content and is displayed on the browser to user or visitor.
It contains more than one web pages that contain information.	It is a single document display on the browser.
It is a combination of web pages created using HTML and CSS.	Information is usually written in HTML language.
It is a place used to display content.	It is content displayed on the website.
It includes content about several entities.	It includes content or information about a single entity.
It can be accessed using HTTP, DNS (Domain Name System) protocols.	It can be accessed through web browser.
There is no such extension included in the URL of the website.	URL of web page include extension.
It includes web pages, related content and hyperlinks.	It might include text, graphics, hyperlinks, etc.
They are used to establish credibility as business and also to increase the positive impression about the company or business that in turn increase user experience.	They are used to provide information with related pictures, videos to users.

13. Discuss the functioning of a web server with its explanation.

Ans. A web server is a program that runs on a computer connected to the Internet. It is simply a computer with an Internet connection that runs software designed to send out HTML, DHTML, XML or Java based pages and other file formats such as multimedia files.

A web server provides four major functions:
 (i) Surfing web pages.
 (ii) Running gateway programs and returning output.
 (iii) Controlling access to the server.
 (iv) Monitoring and logging server access statistics.

14. What do you understand by the term chatting?

Ans. Chatting is the online textual or multimedia conversation. It is widely interactive text based communication process that takes place over the Internet. Chat with people using the Internet is somewhat similar to using the telephone for the same purpose. Chatting, i.e. a virtual means of communication that involves the sending and receiving of messages, share audio and video between users located in any part of the world.

In chatting, you type a message in your chatbox, which is immediately received by the recipient, then the recipient type a message in response to your message which is instantly received by you.

15. Distinguish between server and web server.

Ans. Differences between server and web server are as follows

Server	Web Server
These servers arrange the run environment for enterprises applications.	These servers arrange the run environment for web applications.
These servers utilise more resources.	These servers utilise less resources.
In this server, multi-threading is supported.	In this server, multi-threading is not supported.

• Long Answer Type Questions

16. Define WWW.

Ans. World Wide Web (WWW) or Web, the leading information retrieval service of the Internet (the worldwide computer network). The Web gives users access to a vast array of documents that are connected to each other by means of hypertext or hypermedia links (i.e. hyperlinks), electronic connections that link related pieces of information in order to allow a user easy access to them.

It supports various types of application such as

Multimedia Information It includes different types of movies, music, pictures, graphics, sounds, text, etc.

HyperText Information It includes the links of different types of information resources.

Graphical User Interface (GUI) A user can point/click on the graphical icon to request any information instead of typing in text commands.

World Wide Web is based on client/server software design. A client/server software design requires two types of software to work in a communication environment.

 (i) **Client Software** It is a type of software, which is used by a client (or a user) to request some information from web server, e.g. Web browsers.

 (ii) **Server Software** It is a type of software, which is used by the server to answer the request and provide the required information, e.g. Microsoft, Oracle, etc. It is possible to use your local computer as a server but usually, you want to have a fixed server, which runs 24×7 hours. So, more advanced and large systems are used as a server instead of local computers.

17. Define Voice over Internet Protocol (VoIP). Also, explain its advantages. **[NCERT]**

Ans. VoIP is an IP telephony term for a set of facilities used to manage the delivery of voice information over Internet. It enables a user to make cheap telephone calls over a broadband Internet connection, instead of using a regular telephone service.

A major advantage of VoIP is that avoids the tolls charged by ordinary telephone service. A user can make a call locally or in other parts of US or Canada, or anywhere else in the world, eliminating long distance fees by using a VoIP service.

The concept of VoIP is used in wireless LAN networks and sometimes referred to as WVoIP, VoFI, VoWi-Fi and Wi-Fi VoIP.

Advantages of VoIP
 (i) The biggest single advantage of VoIP has over standard telephone systems is low cost.
 (ii) Using services such as true VoIP, subscribers can call one another at no cost to other party.
 (iii) Routing phone calls over existing data networks eliminate the need for separate voice and data networks.
 (iv) The ability to transmit more than one telephone call over a single broadband connection.
 (v) VoIP consists advance telephone features, e.g. call routing, screen POP and IVR.

18. What is website? Also, write its components.

Ans. A website is a collection of digital documents, primarily HTML files, that are linked together and that exist on the web under the same domain.

A website displays related information on a specific topic. Each website is accessed by its own address known as URL (Uniform Resource Locator).

Components of a website
 (i) **Web host** Group of linked web pages qualify to be called a website only when hosted on a web server.
 (ii) **Address** This is the address of the website (also called URL of the website).
 (iii) **Home page** Every website has a home page. It is the first web page that appears when viewers go to a website.
 (iv) **Design** It is the overall look and feel the website has a result of proper use and integration elements like nevigation menus, layout etc.
 (v) **Content** All the web pages contained in the website together make up the content of the website.
 (vi) **Navigation Structure** The navigation structure of a website is order of the pages, the collection of what

links to what. Usually it is held together by atleast one navigation menu.

19. Differentiate between absolute URL and relative URL.

Ans. (i) **Absolute URL** It is the type of URL, which uses the complete web path of a file to provide the location of the resource, i.e. they provide the actual domain name.

e.g. "http://www.oracle.sun.com/en/index.html"

(ii) **Relative URL** It is the type of URL that defines the path of an URL on a domain, without including the domain name. Relative URLs are more convenient because they are short in length, more portable in website maintenance.

e.g. We specified only ".../images/house.png"

20. What is the utility of a web server? Write about the services provided by web server.

Ans. A web server is a program that runs on a computer connected to the Internet.

It is simply a computer with an Internet connection that runs software designed to send out HTML, DHTML, XML or Java based pages and other file formats such as multimedia files. Web server can refer to either the hardware or software or combination of both which helps to deliver web content that can be accessed through the Internet.

The primary function of a web server is to deliver web pages on the request of client using the HTTP. This means delivery of HTML documents and any additional content that may be included in a document such as images, style sheets and scripts.

A web server provides four major functions:

(i) Serving web pages.

(ii) Running gateway programs and returning output.

(iii) Controlling access to the server.

(iv) Monitoring and logging server access statistics.

Chapter Test

Multiple Choice Questions

1. Which of the following project was created by the National Science Foundation?
(a) NSFNet
(b) WWW
(c) ARPANET
(d) CERN Net

2. Which of the following is not a part of the URL?
(a) WWW
(b) Domain name
(c) Top-level domain
(d) Client workstation

3. The basic purpose of URL is to locate
(a) web server
(b) IP address
(c) web page
(d) node

4. Which web page uses scripting languages to display changing content on the web page?
(a) Static web page
(b) Hybrid web page
(c) Dynamic web page
(d) None of these

5. The space provided by a service provider to store website data is called ....
(a) webspace
(b) cloud computing
(c) web hosting
(d) web store

Short Answer Type Questions

6. How to host a website?

7. How will you change the browser setting in opera?

Long Answer Type Questions

8. Write the process to install the add-ons.

9. Distinguish between chat and E-mail.

Answers

Multiple Choice Questions

1. (a)   2. (d)   3. (a)   4. (c)   5. (c)

For Detailed Solutions
Scan the code

CBSE Term II
Informatics Practices XII

Practice Papers
1-3

Practice Paper 1*
(Solved)

General Instructions

■ Time : 2 Hours
■ Max. Marks : 35

1. There are 9 questions in the question paper. All questions are compulsory.
2. Question no. 1 is a Case Based Question, which has five MCQs. Each question carries one mark.
3. Question no. 2-6 are Short Answer Type Questions. Each question carries 3 marks.
4. Question no. 7-9 are Long Answer Type Questions. Each question carries 5 marks.
5. There is no overall choice. However, internal choices have been provided in some questions. Students have to attempt only one of the alternatives in such questions.

** As exact Blue-print and Pattern for CBSE Term II exams is not released yet. So the pattern of this paper is designed by the author on the basis of trend of past CBSE Papers. Students are advised not to consider the pattern of this paper as official, it is just for practice purpose.*

1. Direction *Read the following passage and answer the questions that follows*

Web server is a special computer system running on HTTP through web pages. The web page is a medium to carry data from one computer system to another. The working of the web server starts from the client or user. The client sends their request through the web browser to the web server. Web server takes this request, processes it and then sends back processed data to the client. The server gathers all of our web page information and sends it to the user, which we see on our computer system in the form of a web page. When the client sends a request for processing to the web server, a domain name and IP address are important to the web server. The domain name and IP address are used to identify the user on a large network.

(i) Web servers are
    (a) IP addresses   (b) computer systems
    (c) web pages of a site   (d) a medium to carry data from one computer to another

(ii) What does the web server need to send back information to the user?
    (a) Home address   (b) Domain name
    (c) IP address   (d) Both (b) and (c)

(iii) What is the full form of HTTP?
    (a) HyperText Transfer Protocol   (b) HyperText Transfer Procedure
    (c) Hyperlink Transfer Protocol   (d) Hyperlink Transfer Procedure

(iv) The .... translates Internet domain and host names to IP address.
    (a) domain name system   (b) routing information protocol
    (c) Internet relay chat   (d) network time protocol

(v) Computer that requests the resources or data from another computer is called as ....
    (a) server   (b) client
    (c) Both (a) and (b)   (d) None of these

2. Write a output for SQL queries (i) to (iii), which are based on the table Student given below:

Table : Student

RollNo	Name	Class	DOB	Gender	City	Marks
1	Nanda	X	06-06-1995	M	Agra	551
2	Saurabh	XII	07-05-1993	M	Mumbai	462
3	Sonal	XI	06-05-1994	F	Delhi	400
4	Trisla	XII	08-08-1995	F	Mumbai	450
5	Sohan	XII	08-10-1995	M	Delhi	369
6	Marisla	XI	12-12-1994	F	Dubai	250
7	Neha	X	08-12-1995	F	Moscow	377
8	Nishant	X	12-06-1995	M	Moscow	489

(i) `SELECT COUNT(*), City FROM Student GROUP BY City HAVING COUNT(*)>1;`

(ii) `SELECT MAX(DOB),MIN(DOB) FROM Student;`

(iii) `SELECT NAME,GENDER FROM Student WHERE City= "Delhi";`

Or Consider the following table Games. Write SQL commands for the following statements.

Table: Games

GCode	GameName	Type	Number	PrizeMoney	ScheduleDate
101	Carom Board	Indoor	2	5000	23/01/2004
102	Badminton	Outdoor	2	12000	12/12/2003
103	Table Tennis	Indoor	4	8000	14/02/2004
105	Chess	Indoor	2	9000	01/01/2004
108	Lawn Tennis	Outdoor	4	25000	19/03/2004

(i) To display the details of those Games, which are having PrizeMoney more than 7000.

(ii) To display sum of PrizeMoney for each Type of Games.

(iii) To display the total number of games available in the above table Games.

3. Differentiate between DDL comand and DML command.

Or Differentiate between CHAR data type and VARCHAR data type.

4. State any two differences between single-row functions and multiple-row functions.

Or What is the difference between the ORDER BY clause and GROUP BY clause.

5. Write the short note on

(i) DAYOFWEEK( )   (ii) DAYOFYEAR ( )

6. Consider the following EMP and DEPARTMENT tables. Write the SQL queries for (i) to (iv) and outputs for SQL queries (v) to (viii).

Table : EMP

EMPNO	ENAME	SEX	DOB	DOJ	DEPTCODE
101	Ram	M	1990-05-02	2012-01-02	D01
102	Aman	M	1992-03-01	2013-02-04	D03
103	Diya	F	1989-01-04	2011-01-06	D04
106	Sandeep	M	1993-04-06	2015-01-03	D02
105	Varun	M	1995-07-08	2014-02-04	D05
107	Komal	F	1994-03-02	2013-03-06	D01
104	Priyanka	F	1995-02-01	2012-02-07	D01

Table : DEPARTMENT

DEPT CODE	DEPTNAME	PLACE
D01	CSE	MUMBAI
D02	IT	KOLKATA
D04	MEDIA	DELHI
D03	HR	MUMBAI
D05	SALES	DELHI

(i) To display EMPNO, ENAME, SEX from the table EMP in descending order of EMPNO

(ii) To display the records of all female employee from the table EMP.

(iii) To display the EMPNO and ENAME of those employees from the table EMP who are joined between '2011-01-01' and '2013-01-01'.

(iv) To count the number of male employees who have borned before '1994-01-01'

(v) `SELECT COUNT(*), DEPTCODE FROM EMP GROUP BY DEPTCODE HAVING COUNT > 1;`

(vi) `SELECT COUNT(DISTINCT DEPTNAME) FROM DEPARTMENT;`

(vii) `SELECT ENAME, DEPTNAME FROM EMP E, DEPARTMENT D WHERE E.DEPTCODE = D.DEPTCODE AND EMPNO < 104;`

(viii) `SELECT MIN(DOJ) MAX(DOB) FROM EMP;`

7. Given a table Bookhouse, write SQL query for part (i) to (v).

Table : Bookhouse

No	Title	Author	Subject	Publisher	Qty	Price
1	Data Structure	Lips Chute	DS	McGraw	4	217.00
2	DOS Guide	Nortron	OS	PHI	3	175.00
3	Turbo C++	Robort Lafore	Prog	Galgotia	5	270.00
4	Dbase Dummies	Palmer	DBMS	PustakM	7	130.00
5	Mastering Windows	Cowart	OS	BPB	1	225.00
6	Computer Studies	French	FND	Galgotia	2	75.00
7	COBOL	Stern	Prog	John W	4	1000.00
8	Guide Network	Freed	NET	Zpress	3	200.00
9	Basic for Beginners	Norton	Prog	BPB	3	40.00
10	Advanced Pascal	Schildt	Prog	McGraw	4	350.00

(i) Display the title of all books with price between 100 and 300.

(ii) Display title and author of all the books having type "Prog" and published by BPB.

(iii) Display number of books and average price for each type of publisher.

(iv) Display title, price in descending order of price.

(v) Display all the books where title starts with "D" and qty is more than 3.

Or Given a table Order, write SQL query for part (i) to (v).

Table : Order

Orderno	Orderdate	CName	Cloc	Orders(in ₹)	Payments (in ₹)
1	12/02/2008	Avlon	Delhi	100000	90000
2	21/11/2008	Parason	Jaipur	230000	230000
3	15/10/2008	Trident	Raipur	120000	100000
4	13/01/2008	Avlon	Jaipur	240000	240000
5	17/07/2008	Trident	Delhi	340000	310000
6	16/06/2008	Nalco	Chennai	140000	140000

(i) Display the name of companies.

(ii) Insert a new row of data as (7,19/02/2007,Nike,Delhi,70000,140000)

(iii) Display the maximum and minimum orders placed for each city.

(iv) Find number of companies and average orders order by Cloc.

(v) List all orders given between 01/01/2008 to 12/10/2008.

8. Answer the following questions.

(i) Write MySQL command that will be used to open an already existing database "CONTACT".

(ii) The Doc_name column of a table Hospital is given below:

Doc_name
Avinash
Hariharan
Vinayak
Deepak
Sanjeev

Based on the above information , find the output of the following queries.

(a) `SELECT Doc_name FROM Hospital WHERE Doc_name LIKE '%v';`

(b) `SELECT Doc_name FROM Hospital WHERE Doc_name LIKE '%e%';`

(iii) A table "Transport" in a database has degree 3 and cardinality 8. What is the number of rows and columns in it?

(iv) Define the degree and cardinality of a relation. Observe the following table and find the degree and cardinality of the given table.

Book Id	ISBN	Book Name	Author	Publication	Price	QTY
1001	123	Java	R. Kumar	Arihant	250	50
1002	124	C++	S. Singh	Bharti	350	25
1003	125	OOP	M. Khan	Navbharat	220	10
1004	126	Dot Net	R. Chand	Kataria	230	20
1005	127	DBMS	Korth	McGraw	500	10

(v) Observe the following table carefully and write the names of the most appropriate columns, which can be considered as (a) Candidate keys and (b) Primary key

Code	Item	Qty	Price	Transaction Date
1001	Plastic Folder 14"	100	3400	2014-12-14
1004	Pen Stand Standard	200	4500	2015-01-31
1005	Stapler Mini	250	1200	2015-02-28
1009	Punching Machine Small	200	1400	2015-03-12
1003	Stapler Big	100	1500	2015-02-02

Or Write SQL queries for (i) to (iv) and find the output for (v).

Table : VEHICLE

VCODE	VEHICLETYPE	PERKM
V01	VOLVO BUS	150
V02	AC DELUXE BUS	125
V03	ORDINARY BUS	80
V05	SUV	30
V04	CAR	18

Note PERKM is Freight Charges per kilometre

Table : TRAVEL

CNO	CNAME	TRAVELDATE	KM	VCODE	NOP
101	K. Niwal	2015-12-13	200	V01	32
103	Fredrick Sym	2016-03-21	120	V03	45
105	Hitesh Jain	2016-04-23	450	V02	42
102	Ravi Anish	2016-01-13	80	V02	40
107	John Malina	2015-02-10	65	V04	2
104	Sahanubhuti	2016-01-28	90	V05	4
106	Ramesh Jaya	2016-04-06	100	V01	25

Note KM is Kilometres travelled
NOP is number of passengers travelled in vehicle.

(i) To display CNO, CNAME, TRAVELDATE from the table TRAVEL in descending order of CNO.

(ii) To display the CNAME of all the customers from the table TRAVEL who are travelling by vehicle with code V01 or V02.

(iii) To display the CNO and CNAME of those customers from the table TRAVEL who travelled between '2015-12-31' and '2015-05-01'.

(iv) To display all the details from table TRAVEL for the customers, who have travel distance more than 120 KM in ascending order of NOP.

(v)
```
SELECT COUNT(*), VCODE FROM TRAVEL
GROUP BY VCODE HAVING COUNT(*)>1;
```

9. WeAtWork consultants are setting up a secured network for their office campus at Gurgaon for their day-to-day office and web-based activities. They are planning to have connectivity between 3 buildings and the head office situated in Mumbai. Answer the questions (i) to (v) after going through the building positions in the campus and other details, which are given below:

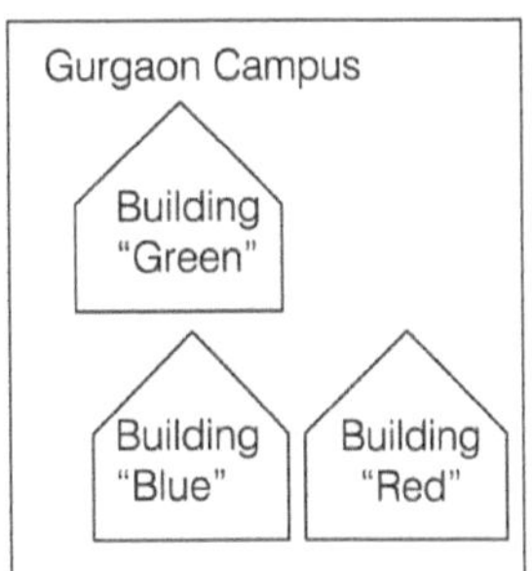

Distance between various buildings

Building "GREEN to Building "RED"	110 m
Building "GREEN" to Building "BLUE"	45 m
Building "BLUE" to Building "RED"	65 m
Building "CAMPUS" to "HEAD OFFICE"	1760 km

Number of computers

Building "GREEN"	32
Building "RED"	150
Building "BLUE"	45
HEAD OFFICE	10

(i) Suggest the most suitable place (i.e. building) to house the server of this organization. Also, give a reason to justify your suggested location.

(ii) Suggest a network device needed to connect GREEN and RED building by UTP cable.

(iii) Suggest the device to connect all computer in each building.

    (a) Switch   (b) Repeater   (c) Router

(iv) The organization is planning to provide a high speed link with its head office situated in "MUMBAI" using a wired connection. Which of the following cables will be most suitable for this?

    (a) Optical fibre   (b) Co-axial cable   (c) Ethernet cable

(v) Suggest the most appropriate media to connect Head Office to new office which is planning to setup inside Arabian Sea where it is not possible to lay cables.

Or Write the short note on the following:

    (i) Web server   (ii) Purpose of cookies   (iii) Mesh topology

EXPLANATIONS

1. (i) (*b*) Web servers are computer systems.

That means a web server is computer software and hardware that accepts requests *via* HTTP, the network protocol created to distribute web content or its secure variant HTTPs.

(ii) (*d*) Domain name and IP address need to send back information to the user.

(iii) (*a*) HTTP stands for Hyper Text Transfer Protocol. It specifies how to transfer hypertext (linked web documents) between two computers.

(iv) (*a*) Domain name system is the way the Internet domain names are stored and translated to IP addresses. The domain name system matches the name of website to IP addresses of the website.

(v) (*b*) Computer that requests the resources or data from other computer is known as client. Client computer always make use of the software or hardware in which the service is made by the server.

2. (i)
```
+----------+---------+
: COUNT(*) : City    :
+----------+---------+
:    2     : Mumbai  :
:    2     : Delhi   :
:    2     : Moscow  :
+----------+---------+
```

(ii)
```
+------------+------------+
: MAX(DOB)   : MIN(DOB)   :
+------------+------------+
:08-12-1995  :07-05-1993  :
+------------+------------+
```

(iii)
```
+----------+----------+
: Name     : Gender   :
+----------+----------+
: Sonal    :   F      :
+----------+----------+
: Sohan    :   M      :
+----------+----------+
```

Or (i)
```
SELECT*FROM Games WHERE PrizeMoney >
7000;
```

(ii)
```
SELECT SUM(PrizeMoney), Type FROM Games
GROUP BY Type;
```

(iii)
```
SELECT COUNT(GameName) FROM Games;
```

3. Differences between DDL and DML commands are as follows

Key	DDL	DML
Stands for	DDL stands for Data Definition Language.	DML stands for Data Manipulation Language.
Usage	DDL statements are used to create database, schema, constraints, tables etc.	DML statement is used to insert, update or delete the records.
Classification	DDL has no further classification.	DML is further classified into procedural DML and non-procedural DML.
Commands	CREATE, DROP, RENAME and ALTER.	INSERT, UPDATE and DELETE.

Or Differences between CHAR and VARCHAR data types are as follows

CHAR Data Type	VARCHAR Data Type
Its full name is CHARACTER.	Its full name is VARIABLE CHARACTER.
It stores values in fixed lengths and are padded with space characters to match the specified length.	VARCHAR stores values in variable length along with 1-byte or 2-byte length prefix and are not padded with any characters.
It can hold a maximum of 255 characters.	It can hold a maximum of 65,535 characters.
It uses static memory allocation.	It uses dynamic memory allocation.

4. Two main differences between single-row functions and multiple-row functions are as follows

Single-row functions	Multiple-row functions
Single-row functions are the one who work on single row and return one output per row.	Multiple-row functions work upon group of rows and return one result for the complete set of rows.
e.g. LOWER, UPPER, SUBSTR, LENGTH, etc.	e.g. COUNT, MIN, MAX, AVG, SUM, etc.

Or The ORDER BY clause is used to show the contents of a table/relation in a sorted manner with respect to the column mentioned after the ORDER BY clause. The contents of the column can be arranged in ascending or descending order.

The GROUP BY clause is used to group rows in a given column and then apply an aggregate function e.g. MAX(), MIN() etc., on the entire group.

5. (i) **DAYOFWEEK ( )**

This function returns the week day number (1= Sunday, 2= Monday, ..., 7 = Saturday) for a date specified as an argument.

Syntax DAYOFWEEK (date/column_name)

(ii) **DAYOFYEAR( )**

This function returns day of the year for a given date in numeric format. The return value is within the range of 1 to 366.

Syntax DAYOFYEAR (date/column_name)

6. (i) SELECT EMPNO, ENAME, SEX FROM EMP ORDER BY DESC;

(ii) SELECT * FROM EMP WHERE SEX = 'F';

(iii) SELECT EMPNO, ENAME FROM EMP WHERE DOJ BETWEEN '2011-01-01' AND '2013-01-01';

(iv) SELECT COUNT(EMPNO) WHERE SEX= 'M' AND DOJ < '1994-01-01';

(v)

COUNT (*)	DEPTCODE
3	D01

(vi)

COUNT(DISTINCT DEPTNAME)
5

(vii)

ENAME	DEPTNAME
Ram	CSE
Diya	MEDIA
Aman	HR

(viii)

MIN (DOJ)	MAX (DOB)
2011-01-06	1995-07-08

7. (i) SELECT Title FROM Bookhouse WHERE Price BETWEEN 100 AND 300;

(ii) SELECT Title, Author FROM Bookhouse WHERE Subject='Prog' AND Publisher='BPB';

(iii) SELECT COUNT(*), AVG(Price) FROM Bookhouse GROUP BY Publisher;

(iv) SELECT Title, Price FROM Bookhouse ORDER BY Price DESC;

(v) SELECT * FROM Bookhouse WHERE Title LIKE 'D%' AND Qty>3;

Or (i) SELECT DISTINCT(CName) FROM Order;

(ii) INSERT INTO Order VALUES(8,'19/02/2007', 'Nike', 'Delhi',70000, 140000);

(iii) SELECT Cloc, MAX (Orders), MIN (Orders) FROM Order GROUP BY Cloc;

(iv) SELECT Cloc, COUNT(Cloc), AVG(Orders) FROM Order GROUP BY Cloc;

(v) SELECT * FROM Order WHERE Orderdate>'01/01/2008' AND Orderdate<'12/10/2008';

8. (i) USE CONTACT;

(ii) (a)

Doc_name
Sanjeev

(b)

Doc_name
Deepak
Sanjeev

(iii) Number of rows: 8

Number of columns: 3

(iv) **Degree of relation** It represents the total number of columns in a relation.

The degree of the given table is 7.

Cardinality It represents the total number of row in a relation. The cardinality of the given table is 5.

(v) (a) Candidate key - Code, Item

(b) Primary key - Code

Or

(i) SELECT CNO, CNAME, TRAVELDATE FROM TRAVEL A, VEHICLE B WHERE A.VCODE = B.VCODE AND ORDER BY CNO DESC;

(ii) SELECT CNAME FROM TRAVEL WHERE VCODE = "V01" OR VCODE = "V02";

(iii) SELECT CNO, CNAME FROM TRAVEL WHERE TRAVELDATE BETWEEN '2015-12-31' AND '2015-05-01';

(iv) SELECT * FROM TRAVEL WHERE KM>120 ORDER BY NOP;

(v)

COUNT (*)	VCODE
2	V01
2	V02

9. (i) In building RED as it has maximum number of computers.

(ii) Repeater

(iii) (*a*) Switch

(iv) (*a*) Optical fibre

(v) Microwave

Or (i) **Web Server** A web server is software and hardware that uses the HyperText Transfer Protocol and some other protocols to respond to client requests made over the World Wide Web. The main job of a web server is to display website content through storing, processing and delivering web pages to users.

Web server hardware is connected to the Internet and allows data to be exchanged with other connected devices, while web server software controls how a user accesses hosted files. The web server process is an example of client/server model.

(ii) **Purpose of Cookies** Cookies are text files with small pieces of data — like a username and password — that are used to identify our computer as we use a computer network. Specific cookies known as HTTP cookies are used to identify specific users and improve our web browsing experience. Data stored in a cookie is created by the server upon our connection. This data is labeled with an ID unique to us and our computer. When the cookie is exchanged between our computer and the network server, the server reads the ID and knows what information need to specifically serve to us.

(iii) **Mesh Topology** Mesh topology is an arrangement of the network in which computers are interconnected with each other through various redundant connections. There are multiple paths from one computer to another computer. It does not contain the switch, hub or any central computer which acts as a central point of communication.

The Internet is an example of the mesh topology. Mesh topology is mainly used for WAN implementations where communication failures are a critical concern. Mesh topology is mainly used for wireless networks.

Mesh topology can be formed by using the formula:

Number of cables = $(n*(n-1))/2$;

where, n is the number of nodes that represents the network.

Practice Paper 2*
(Solved)

General Instructions

- **Time :** 2 Hours
- **Max. Marks :** 35

1. There are 9 questions in the question paper. All questions are compulsory.
2. Question no. 1 is a Case Based Question, which has five MCQs. Each question carries one mark.
3. Question no. 2-6 are Short Answer Type Questions. Each question carries 3 marks.
4. Question no. 7-9 are Long Answer Type Questions. Each question carries 5 marks.
5. There is no overall choice. However, internal choices have been provided in some questions. Students have to attempt only one of the alternatives in such questions.

** As exact Blue-print and Pattern for CBSE Term II exams is not released yet. So the pattern of this paper is designed by the author on the basis of trend of past CBSE Papers. Students are advised not to consider the pattern of this paper as official, it is just for practice purpose.*

1. **Direction** *Read the following passage and answer the questions that follows*

   Consider the table TRAVEL as given below:

   Table : Travel

No	Name	Tdate	Km	Code	NOP
101	Janish Kin	2015–11–13	200	101	32
103	Vedika Sahai	2016–04–21	100	103	45
105	Tarun Ram	2016–03–23	350	102	42
102	John Fen	2016–02–13	90	102	40
107	Ahmed Khan	2015–01–10	75	104	2
104	Raveena	2016–05–28	80	105	4

   Basis the above table information, answer the following questions.

   (i) Write query to give the output as:

   ```
   +-------+--------------+--------------+-------+
   |  No   |  Name        |  Tdate       |  Km   |
   +-------+--------------+--------------+-------+
   |  101  |  Janish Kin  |  2015-11-13  |  200  |
   |  105  |  Tarun Ram   |  2016-03-23  |  350  |
   +-------+--------------+--------------+-------+
   ```

   (a) SELECT * FROM Travel WHERE Km>200;
   (b) SELECT * FROM Travel WHERE Km>=200;
   (c) SELECT No, Name, Tdate, Km FROM Travel WHERE Km>=200;
   (d) SELECT No, Name, Tdate, Km FROM Travel WHERE Km BETWEEN 200 AND 350;

(ii) Write query to display maximum Km from Travel table.
   (a) SELECT MAX (Km) FROM Travel;
   (b) SELECT MAXIMUM(Km) FROM Travel;
   (c) SELCT HIGHEST (Km) FROM Travel;
   (d) None of the above

(iii) Akhil has given the following command to arrange the data in ascending order of date.

```
SELECT * FROM Travel WHERE ORDER BY Tdate;
```

But he is not getting the desired result. Help him by choosing the correct command.
   (a) `SELECT * FROM Travel ORDER BY Tdate;`
   (b) `SELECT * FROM Travel IN ASC;`
   (c) `SELECT Tdate FROM Travel ORDER BY Tdate;`
   (d) None of the above

(iv) Choose the correct query to count the number of codes in each code type from Travel table?
   (I) `SELECT COUNT(Code) FROM Travel ;`
   (II) `SELECT Code,COUNT(Code) FROM Travel GROUP BY Code;`
   (III) `SELECT code,COUNT( DISTINCT Code) FROM Travel;`
   (IV) `SELECT Code, COUNT( DISTINCT Code) FROM Travel GROUP BY Code;`

Choose the correct option.
   (a) Both (II) and (III)   (b) Both (II) and (IV)   (c) Both (I) and (III)   (d) Only (II)

(v) Choose the correct command to display the name of the traveller whose travel date is in year 2016.
   (a) `SELECT Name, Tdate FROM Travel WHERE YEAR(Tdate)=2016 ;`
   (b) `SELECT Name, Tdate FROM Travel WHERE Tdate=2016;`
   (c) `SELECT Name, Tdate FROM Travel WHERE YFAR(Tdate)= =2016;`
   (d) `SELECT Name, MAX(Tdate) FROM Travel ;`

2. What is the use of GROUP BY clause? Give an example.

Or What do you understand by degree and cardinality of a table? Give an example.

3. Given below a table Bookhouse, write SQL query for part (i) to (v).

Table : Bookhouse

No	Title	Author	Subject	Publisher	Qty	Price
1	Data Structure	Lips chute	DS	McGraw	4	217.00
2	DOS Guide	Nortron	OS	PHI	3	175.00
3	Turbo C++	Robort Lafore	Prog	Galgotia	5	270.00
4	Dbase Dummies	Palmer	DBMS	PustakM	7	130.00
5	Mastering Windows	Cowart	OS	BPB	1	225.00
6	Computer Studies	French	FND	Galgotia	2	75.00
7	COBOL	Stern	Prog	John W	4	1000.00
8	Guide Network	Freed	NET	Zpress	3	200.00
9	Basic for Beginners	Norton	Prog	BPB	3	40.00
10	Advanced Pascal	Schildt	Prog	McGraw	4	350.00

(i) Display publisher wise total stock value (Qty * Price).

(ii) Display title of the book which is costliest.

(iii) Display number of books and total price for each type of publisher.

(iv) Display all the books where subject starts with "D" and qty is less than 3.

(v) Display all information of books whose price starts with 2.

Or Describe different kinds of SQL command with proper examples.

4.

Table : Employee

Eno	Ename	Job	Salary	Dept
101	Anupam	Programmer	5000	10
102	Mahesh kumar	Editor	2500	20
103	Dinesh	Programmer	2700	10

Write SQL queries for the following questions.

(i) Display Eno, Ename and Job in descending order of Eno.

(ii) Find the maximum salary of department 10.

(iii) Count the total employees working in each department.

5. Answer the following:

(i) Write SQL command used to display the structure of a table.

(ii) Mr. lames created a table Client with 2 rows and 4 columns. He added 2 more rows to it and deleted one column. What is the cardinality and degree of the table Client?

(iii) In MySQL, Reena and Zebi are getting the following output of SELECT statement on a table Employee.

```
+ - - - - - - - - - + - - - - - - - - +
|  Reena            |  Zebi          |
+ - - - - - - - - - + - - - - - - - -+
|  Lucknow          |  Lucknow       |
|  Delhi            |  Delhi         |
|  Mumbai           |  Mumbai        |
|  Delhi            |  Kanpur        |
|  Kanpur           |                |
|  Delhi            |                |
+ - - - - - - - - - + - - - - - - - -+
```

Which keyword has Zebi used with a SELECT statement to get the above output?

6. What will be the output of the following command?

(i) `SELECT POWER(10,2)`

(ii) `SELECT ROUND(14.4743, 1)`

Or Consider the decimal number x with value 8459.2654. Write commands in SQL.

(i) To round it off to a whole number.

(ii) To round it to 2 places before the decimal.

7. What do you mean by network topology? Write different types of topology.

Or Write one advantage each of star and bus topology used in networking. Draw a network layout of bus topology to connect six computers.

8. JNV School at Hyderabad have their offices according to the following diagram. Go through the details and answer the questions that follows.

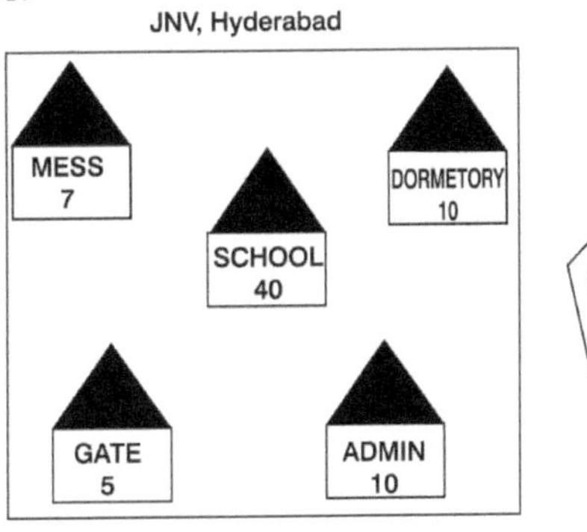

Distance between various wings are given below:

Wings	Distance (in metre)
MESS to SCHOOL	60
MESS to DORMETORY	110
MESS to GATE	65
MESS to ADMIN	130
SCHOOL to DORMETORY	40
SCHOOL to GATE	50
SCHOOL to ADMIN	68
DORMETORY to GATE	115
DORMETORY to ADMIN	100
GATE to ADMIN	65

(i) Name the most suitable wing where the server should be installed. Justify your answer.

(ii) Draw the cable layout to efficiently connect various wings JNV, Hyderabad and also write the topology.

(iii) Suggest a device/software and its placement that would provide data security for the entire network of the School.

(iv) (a) Which device will you suggest to be placed/installed in each of these wings to efficiently connect all the computers within these wings.

   (b) Suggest the placement of a repeater in the network with justification.

(v) Suggest a device and the protocol that shall be needed to provide wireless Internet access to all smartphone/laptop users in the campus of JNV, Hyderabad.

Or Draw the arrangement for connecting five computers in star and mesh topologies.

9. Consider a table "Salesman" with the following data:

Table : Salesman

Sno	Sname	Salary	Bonus	DOJ
A01	Beena Mehta	30000	45.23	29-10-2019
A02	K.L. Sahay	50000	25.34	13-03-2018
B03	Nisha Thakkar	30000	35.00	18-03-2017
B04	Leela Yadav	80000	NULL	31-12-2018
C05	Gautam Gola	20000	NULL	23-01-1989
C06	Trapti Garg	70000	12.37	15-06-1987
D07	Neena Sharma	50000	27.89	18-03-1999

Write SQL queries using SQL functions to perform the following operations.

(i) Display salesman name and bonus after rounding off to zero decimal places.

(ii) Display the position of occurrence of the string "ta" in salesman names.

(iii) Display the four characters from salesman name starting from second character.

(iv) Display the month name for the date of join of salesman.

(v) Display the name of the weekday for the date of join of salesman.

Or A departmental store MyStore is considering to maintain their inventory using SQL to store the data. As a database administer, Abhay has decided that :

• Name of the database - MyStore

• Name of the table - Store

- The attributes of Store are as follows:

ItemNo-numeric

ItemName-character of size 20

Scode-numeric

Quantity-numeric

Table : Store

ItemNo	ItemName	Scode	Quantity
2005	Sharpener Classic	23	60
2003	Ball Pen 0.25	22	50
2002	Get Pen Premium	21	150
2006	Get Pen Classic	21	250
2001	Eraser Small	22	220
2004	Eraser Big	22	110
2009	Ball Pen 0.5	21	180

(i) Identify the attribute best suitable to be declared as a primary key.

(ii) Write the degree and cardinality of the table Store.

(iii) Insert the following data into the attributes ItemNo, ItemName and Scode respectively in the given table Store.

ItemNo = 2010, ItemName = "Note Book" and Scode = 25

(iv) Abhay want to remove the table Store from the database MyStore.

Which command will he use from the following?

(a) `DELETE FROM Store;`

(b) `DROP TABLE Store;`

(c) `DROP DATABASE MyStore;`

(d) `DELETE Store FROM MyStore;`

(v) Now Abhay wants to display the structure of the table Store, i.e. name of the attributes and their respective data types that he has used in the table. Write the query to display the same.

EXPLANATIONS

1. (i) (c) `SELECT No,Name, Tdate,Km FROM Travel WHERE Km>=200;`
   (ii) (a) `SELECT MAX(Km) FROM Travel;`
   (iii) (a) `SELECT * FROM Travel ORDER BY Tdate;`
   (iv) (d) `SELECT Code,COUNT(Code)FROM TRAVEL GROUP BY Code;`
   (v) (a) `SELECT Name, Tdate FROM Travel WHERE YEAR(Tdate)=2016 ;`

2. The GROUP BY clause is used to group records of a table on the basis of a common value of a column and get a summarised result for the group as per a defined function, e.g. if in a class students belong to different school houses ,then we can count the number of students in each house using a GROUP BY command such as:
   `SELECT COUNT(HOUSE)FROM STUDENT GROUP BY HOUSE;`

   Or **Degree** Number of columns/attributes/fields in a table are called table's degree.

   Cardinality Number of rows/tuples/records in a table are called table's cardinality.

   For example,

Bookno	Name	Author	Price
B01	Good learning	Xion Z.	220
B02	Smile easy	T.Singh	350
B03	I to U	S.Sandeep	250

   Degree is 4 because it has 4 columns and cardinality is 3 because it has 3 rows.

3. (i) `SELECT Publisher, Qty*Price AS Total_Stock_Value FROM Bookhouse GROUP BY Publisher;`
   (ii) `SELECT Title FROM Bookhouse WHERE Price=MAX(Price);`
   (iii) `SELECT COUNT(*), SUM(Price) FROM Bookhouse GROUP BY Publisher;`
   (iv) `SELECT Title FROM Bookhouse WHERE Subject LIKE 'D%' AND Qty<3;`
   (v) `SELECT * FROM Bookhouse WHERE Price LIKE '2%';`

   Or SQL commands are instructions. It is used to communicate with the database. It is also used to perform specific tasks, functions and queries of data. SQL can perform various tasks like create a table, add data to tables, drop the table, modify the table, set permission for users.

   Types of SQL commands are as follows

   (i) **Data Definition Language (DDL)** DDL changes the structure of the table like creating a table, deleting a table, altering a table, etc. All the command of DDL are auto-committed that means it permanently save all the changes in the database.
   Here are some commands that come under DDL:
   CREATE
   ALTER
   DROP
   TRUNCATE

   (ii) **Data Manipulation Language (DML)** DML commands are used to modify the database. It is responsible for all form of changes in the database. The command of DML is not auto-committed that means it cannot permanently save all the changes in the database. They can be rollback.
   Here are some commands that come under DML:
   INSERT
   UPDATE
   DELETE

   (iii) **Data Control Language (DCL)** DCL commands are used to grant and take back authority from any database user.
   Here are some commands that come under DCL:
   GRANT
   REVOKE

4. (i) `SELECT Eno, Ename, Job FROM Employee ORDER BY Eno DESC;`
   (ii) `SELECT MAX(Salary) FROM Employee WHERE Dept=10;`
   (iii) `SELECT COUNT(*), Dept FROM Employee GROUP BY Dept;`

5. (i) The command to display the structure of a table is as follows:
   `DESCRIBE table_name;`
   or `DESC table_name;`

(ii) Cardinality = 4

Degree = 3

where, cardinality are the number of rows and degree is number of columns in a table.

(iii) Zebi has used DISTINCT clause with the SELECT command.

6. (i) 100

(ii) 14.5

Or (i) `SELECT ROUND(8459.2654);`

(ii) `SELECT ROUND(8459.2654,-2);`

7. A network topology is the arrangement with which computer systems or network devices are connected to each other. Topologies may define both physical and logical aspect of the network. Both logical and physical topologies could be same or different in a same network.

There are different types of topology, which are as

Bus Topology In case of bus topology, all devices share single communication line or cable. Bus topology may have problem while multiple hosts sending data at the same time. It is one of the simple forms of networking where a failure of a device does not affect the other devices. But failure of the shared communication line can make all other devices stop functioning.

Star Topology All hosts in star topology are connected to a central device, known as hub device, using a point-to-point connection. i.e. there exists a point-to-point connection between hosts and hub.

As in bus topology, hub acts as single point of failure. If hub fails, connectivity of all hosts to all other hosts fails. Every communication between hosts, takes place through only the hub. Star topology is not expensive as to connect one more host, only one cable is required and configuration is simple.

Tree Topology

This topology divides the network into multiple levels/layers of network. Mainly in LANs, a network is bifurcated into three types of network devices. The lowermost is access-layer where computers are attached. The middle layer is known as distribution layer, which works as mediator between upper layer and lower layer.

The highest layer is known as core layer and is central point of the network. i.e. root of the tree from which all nodes fork. All neighboring hosts have point-to-point connection between them.Similar to the bus topology, if the root goes down, then the entire network suffers even.though it is not the single point of failure. Every connection serves as point of failure, failing of which divides the network into unreachable segment.

Or Advantage of star topology is that it is most reliable as there is a direct connection of every node with the central node or server. Advantage of bus topology is that all nodes are connected through a single length of a cable, so very short cable length is used.

A network layout of bus topology to connect six computers is as follows:

8. (i) SCHOOL, it contains maximum number of computers.

(ii) Star topology

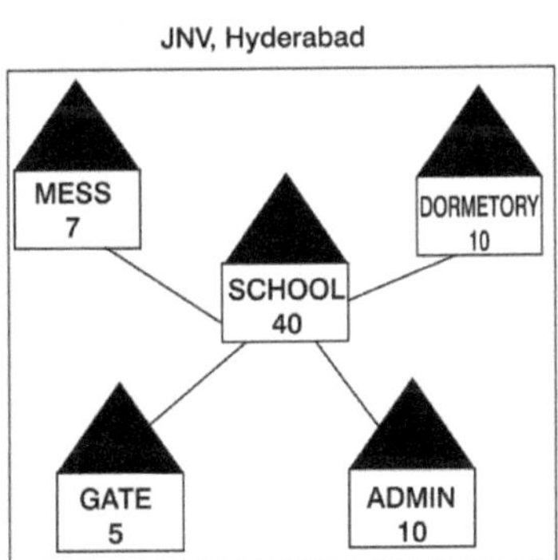

(iii) Firewall should be installed in the SCHOOL where the server is located.

(iv) (a) Hub/Switch

   (b) Repeater should be installed where the distance between the wings is 70 metre or more. As per the above layout no repeater is required.

(v) **Devices** Wi-Fi or WiMAX or Wi-Fi router

   Protocols – 802.11, WAP, 802.16

Or **Star Topology**

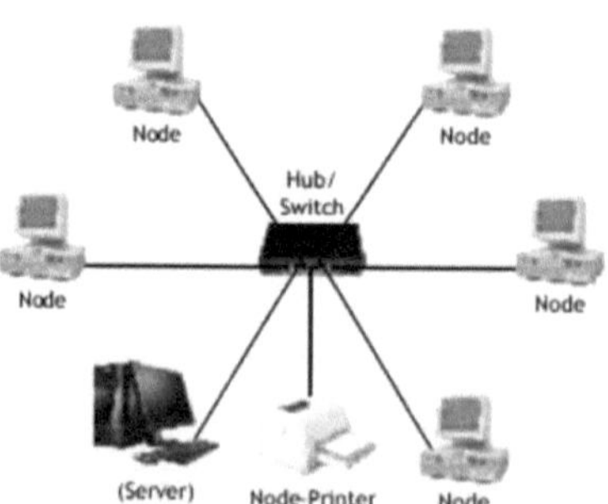

Mesh Topology

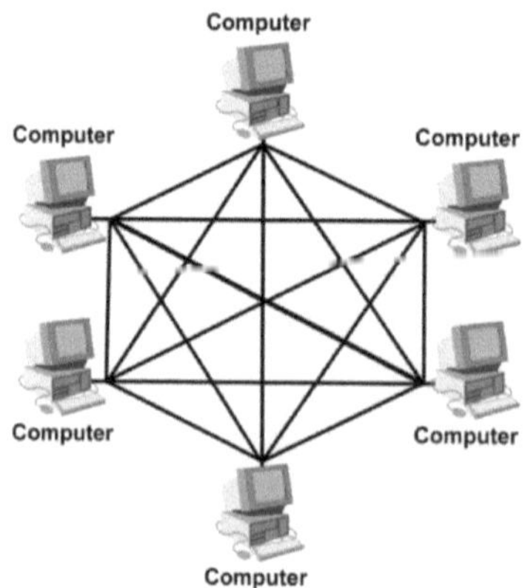

9.
```
 (i) SELECT Sname, ROUND(Bonus,0)FROM Salesman;
 (ii) SELECT INSTR(Sname, "ta") FROM Salesman;
(iii) SELECT MID(Sname,2,4) FROM Salesman;
 (iv) SELECT MONTHNAME(DOJ) FROM Salesman;
  (v) SELECT DAYNAME(DOJ)FROM Salesman;
```

Or (i) ItemNo

   (ii) Degree- 4, Cardinality- 7

```
(iii) INSERT INTO Store VALUES(2010,'Note Book',NULL,25);
 (iv) (b) DROP TABLE Store;
  (v) DESCRIBE Store
      or DESC Store;
```

Practice Paper 3*
(Solved)

1. Direction *Read the following passage and answer the questions that follows*

Consider the table Student as given below :

Table : Student

RollNo	Name	Class	DOB	Gender	City	Marks
1	Anand	XI	06-06-1997	M	Agra	430
2	Chetan	XII	07-05-1994	M	Mumbai	460
3	Geet	XI	06-05-1997	F	Agra	470
4	Priti	XII	08-08-1995	F	Mumbai	492
5	Saniya	XII	08-10-1995	F	Delhi	360
6	Neha	X	08-12-1995	F	Burdwan	324
7	Nishant	X	12-06-1995	M	Burdwan	429

Based on above table information, answer the following questions.

(i) State the command that will give the output as :

```
+--------+
| Name   |
+--------+
| Anand  |
| Chetan |
| Geet   |
| Priti  |
+--------+
```

```
 (I) SELECT Name FROM Student WHERE Class='XI' AND Class='XII';
 (II) SELECT Name FROM Student WHERE NOT Class='XI' AND Class='XII';
 (III) SELECT Name FROM Student WHERE City="Agra" OR City="Mumbai";
 (IV) SELECT Name FROM Student WHERE City IN("Agra", "Mumbai");
```
Choose the correct option.
(a) Both (I) and (II)
(b) Both (III) and (IV)
(c) Any of the options (I), (II) and (IV)
(d) Only (III)

(ii) What will be the output of the following command?
```
SELECT * FROM Student WHERE Gender ="F" AND Class = "XII" ORDER BY Marks;
```

(a)

RollNo	Name	Class	DOB	Gender	City	Marks
1	Priti	XII	08-08-1995	F	Mumbai	492

(b)

RollNo	Name	Class	DOB	Gender	City	Marks
5	Saniya	XII	08-10-1995	F	Delhi	360

(c)

RollNo	Name	Class	DOB	Gender	City	Marks
1	Priti	XII	08-08-1995	F	Mumbai	492
5	Saniya	XII	08-10-1995	F	Delhi	360

(d) None of the above

(iii) Prachi has given the following command to obtain the highest marks:
```
SELECT MAX(Marks) FROM Student WHERE GROUP BY Class;
```

But she is not getting the desired result. Help her by writing the correct command.
```
(a) SELECT MAX(Marks) FROM Student WHERE GROUP BY Class;
(b) SELECT Class, MAX(Marks) FROM Student GROUP BY Marks;
(c) SELECT Class, MAX(Marks) GROUP BY Class FROM Student;
(d) SELECT Class, MAX(Marks) FROM Student GROUP BY Class;
```

(iv) State the command to display the average marks scored by students of each gender who are in class XI.
```
 (I) SELECT Gender, AVG(Marks) FROM Student WHERE Class= "XI" GROUP BY Gender;
 (II) SELECT Gender, AVG(Marks) FROM Student GROUP BY Gender WHERE Class=''XI";
 (III) SELECT Gender, AVG(Marks) GROUP BY Gender FROM Student HAVING Class=''XI";
 (IV) SELECT Gender, AVG(Marks) FROM Student GROUP BY Gender HAVING Class ="XI";
```
Choose the correct option.
(a) Both (II) and (III)   (b) Both (II) and (IV)
(c) Both (I) and (III)   (d) Only (III)

(v) Help Ritesh to write the command to display the name of the youngest student?
```
(a) SELECT Name,MIN(DOB) FROM Student ;
(b) SELECT Name,MAX(DOB) FROM Student ;
(c) SELECT Name,MIN(DOB) FROM Student GROUP BY Name ;
(d) SELECT Name,MAXIMUM(DOB) FROM Student;
```

2. Observe the following table LIST and find the degree and Cardinality of the LIST.

Table: LIST

NO	NAME	EVENTCODE	EVENTNAME
1	Tara Mani	1001	Programming
1	Tara Mani	1002	IT Quiz
2	Jaya Sarkar	1001	Programming
2	Jaya Sarkar	1002	IT Quiz
3	Tarini Trikha	1001	Programming
3	Tarini Trikha	1002	IT Quiz

3. Observe the following table carefully and write the names of the most appropriate columns, which can be considered as (i) candidate keys and (ii) primary key.

Id	Product	Qty	Price	Transaction Date
101	Plastic Folder 12"	100	3400	2014-12-14
104	Pen Stand Standard	200	4500	2015-01-31
105	Stapler Medium	250	1200	2015-02-28
109	Punching Machine Big	200	1400	2015-03-12
103	Stapler Mini	100	1500	2015-02-02

Or Consider the following DEPT and WORKER tables. Write SQL queries for (i) to (iv) and find output for SQL query (v).

Table: DEPT

DCODE	DEPARTMENT	CITY
D01	MEDIA	DELHI
D02	MARKETING	DELHI
D03	INFRASTRUCTURE	MUMBAI
D05	FINANCE	KOLKATA
D04	HUMAN RESOURCE	MUMBAI

Table: WORKER

WNO	NAME	DOJ	DOB	GENDER	DCODE
1001	George K	2013-09-02	1991-09-01	MALE	D01
1002	Ryma Sen	2012-12-11	1990-12-15	FEMALE	D03
1003	Mohitesh	2013-02-03	1987-09-04	MALE	D05
1007	Anil Jha	2014-01-17	1984-10-19	MALE	D04
1004	Manila Sahai	2012-12-09	1986-11-14	FEMALE	D01
1005	R SAHAY	2013-11-18	1987-03-31	MALE	D02
1006	Jaya Priya	2014-06-09	1985-06-23	FEMALE	D05

Note *DOJ refers to Date of Joining and DOB refers to Date of Birth of workers.*

(i) To display WNO, NAME, GENDER from the table WORKER in descending order of WNO.

(ii) To display the NAME of all the FEMALE workers from the table WORKER.

(iii) To display the WNO and NAME of those workers from the table WORKER, who are born between '1987-01-01' and '1991-12-01'.

(iv) To count and display MALE workers who have joined after '1986-01-01'.

(v)
```
        SELECT COUNT(*), DCODE FROM WORKER
        GROUP BY DCODE HAVING COUNT(*)>1;
```

4. Write a SQL command for creating a table 'SUPPLIERS';

Table: SUPPLIERS

Field_Name	Datatype	Size
Product_id	INTEGER	4
Product_Name	CHAR	10
Quantity	INTEGER	10
Price	DECIMAL	7,2
Phone	CHAR	10

Or Consider the following table Vehicles :

Table : Vehicles

V_No	Type	Company	Price	Qty
AW125	Wagon	Maruti	250000	25
J0083	Jeep	Mahindra	4000000	15
S9090	SUV	Mitsubishi	2500000	18
M0892	Mini Van	Datsun	1500000	26
W9760	SUV	Maruti	2500000	18
R2409	Mini Van	Mahindra	350000	15

Basis on above table information, write SQL commands for the following questions.

(i) Display the average price of each type of vehicle having quantity more than 20.

(ii) Count the type of vehicles manufactured by each company.

(iii) Display the total price of all the types of vehicles.

5. (i) Write a query to display current date on your system.

(ii) Display the position of occurrence of string "OR" in the string "CORPORATE LAWYER".

(iii) Mrs. Kumar is using table Students with the following columns:

Rno,AdmNo,Name,Aggregate

She wants to display all information of students in descending order of name and with ascending order of aggregate. She wrote the following SQL query and she did not get the desired result.

```
SELECT * FROM Students ORDER BY Name, Aggregate DESC;
```

Or Predict the output of the following.

(i) `SELECT POW(INSTR("Success@dedication","@"),2);`

(ii) `SELECT MONTH("2020-11-15")*POW(2,3);`

(iii) Mr. Janak is using a table with following columns:

Name, Class, Course_Id, Course_Name

He needs to display name of students, who have not been assigned any stream or have been assigned Course_Name that ends with "economics".

He wrote the following query, which did not give the desired result.

```
SELECT Name, Class FROM Students WHERE Course_Name=NULL OR Course_Name="%economics";
```

Help Mr. Janak to run the query by removing the error and write the correct query.

6. Write the SQL functions which will perform the following operations:

(i) To display the name of the day of the current date.

(ii) To remove spaces from the beginning of a string " Python".

(iii) To display the name of the month e.g. January or February from your date of birth(dob).

(iv) To display the starting position of word "Information" from "Information Technology" .

(v) To compute the power of two numbers a and b .

7. (i) Write the name of the most suitable wireless communication channels for each of the following situations.

(a) Communication between two offices in two different countries.

(b) To transfer the data from one mobile phone to another.

(ii) Mr. Chandervardhan is not able to identify the domain name in the given URL. Identify and write it for him.

http://www.cbsenic.in/aboutus.htm

Or Expand the following abbreviations :

(i) HTTP   (ii) ARPANET

(iii) VPN   (iv) MODEM

(v) TCP/IP

(vi) DNS

8. How is the call quality of a VoIP phone?

Or A company in Mega Enterprises has 4 wings of buildings as shown in the diagram :

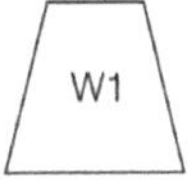

Center to center distances between various buildings:

W3 to W1	-	50m
W1 to W2	-	60m
W2 to W4	-	25m
W4 to W3	-	170m
W3 to W2	-	125m
W1 to W4	-	90m

Number of computers in each of the wing:

W1	-	150
W2	-	15
W3	-	15
W4	-	25

Computers in each wing are networked but wings are not networked. The company has now decided to connect the wings also.

(i) Suggest a most suitable cable layout for the above connections.

(ii) Suggest the most appropriate topology of the connection between the wings.

(iii) The company wants Internet accessibility in all the wings. Suggest a suitable technology.

(iv) Suggest the placement of the following devices with justification if the company wants minimized network traffic.

(a) Repeater

(b) Hub/Switch

(v) The company is planning to link its head office situated in New Delhi with the offices in hilly areas. Suggest a way to connect it economically.

9. Modern Public School is maintaining fees records of students. The database administrator Aman decided that

- Name of the database-School
- Name of the table-Fees
- The attributes of Fees are as follows:

Rollno-numeric

Name-character of size 20

Class-character of size 20

Fees-numeric

Qtr-numeric

Answer any four questions from the following :

(i) Identify the attribute best suitable to be declared as a primary key.

(ii) Write the degree of the table.

(iii) Insert the following data into the attributes Rollno, Name, Class, Fees and Qtr in Fees table.

(iv) Aman want to remove the tablo Fees from the database School.

Which command will he use?

(a) `DELETE FROM Fees;`

(b) `DROP TABLE Fees;`

(c) `DROP DATABASE Fees;`

(d) `DELETE Fees FROM Fees;`

(v) Now, Aman wants to display the structure of the table Fees, i.e. name of the attributes and their respective data types that he has used in the table. Write the query to display the same.

Or Consider the table Sports given below. Write commands in SQL for (i) to (iv) and output for (v) to (viii).

Table : Sports

StudentNo	Class	Name	Game1	Grade1	Game2	Grade2
10	7	Sammer	Cricket	B	Swimming	A
11	8	Sujit	Tennis	A	Skating	C
12	7	Kamal	Swimming	B	Football	B
13	7	Venna	Tennis	C	Tennis	A
14	9	Archana	Basketball	A	Cricket	A
15	10	Arpit	Cricket	A	Athletics	C

(i) Display the names of the students who have grade 'A' in either Game1 or Game2 or both.

(ii) Display the number of students having game 'Cricket'.

(iii) Display the names of students who have same game for both Game1 and Game2.

(iv) Display the games taken by the students whose name starts with 'A'.

(v) `SELECT COUNT(*) FROM Sports;`

(vi) `SELECT DISTINCT Class FROM Sports;`

(vii) `SELECT MAX(Class) FROM Student;`

(viii) `SELECT COUNT(*) FROM Sports GROUP BY Game1;`

EXPLANATIONS

1. (i) (*b*) Both (III) and (IV)

   (ii) (*c*)

```
+ -----+-----+------+------------+------+------+------+
|RollNo| Name| Class|    DOB     |Gender| City |Marks |
+ -----+-----+------+------------+------+------+------+
|  1   |Priti| XII  |08-08-1995  |  F   |Mumbai| 492  |
+ -----+-----+------+------------+------+------+------+
|  5   |Saniya| XII |08-10-1997  |  F   |Delhi | 360  |
+ -----+-----+------+------------+------+------+------+
```

   (iii) (*d*) SELECT Class, MAX(Marks) FROM Student GROUP BY Class;

   (iv) (*b*) Both (II) and (IV)

   (v) (*b*) `SELECT Name,MAX(DOB) FROM Student ;`

2. Degree = 4

   Cardinality = 6

3. (i) Candidate Keys :- Id, Product

   (ii) Primary Key :- Id

Or (i) `SELECT WNO, NAME, GENDER FROM WORKER ORDER BY WNO DESC;`

   (ii) `SELECT NAME FROM WORKER WHERE GENDER = "FEMALE";`

   (iii) `SELECT WNO, NAME FROM WORKER WHERE DOB BETWEEN '1987-01-01' AND '1991-12-01';`

   (iv) `SELECT COUNT(*) FROM WORKER WHERE GENDER = "MALE" AND DOJ > '1986-01-01';`

   (v)

COUNT (*)	DCODE
2	D01
2	D05

4.
```
CREATE TABLE SUPPLIERS
(
Product_id INT(4),
Product_Name CHAR(10),
Quantity INT(10),
Price DECIMAL(7,2),
Phone CHAR(10)
);
```

Or (i) `SELECT Type, AVG(Price) FROM Vehicle GROUP BY Type HAVING Qty > 20;`

   (ii) `SELECT Company, COUNT(DISTINCT Type) FROM Vehicle GROUP BY Company;`

   (iii) `SELECT Type, SUM(Price* Qty) FROM Vehicle GROUP BY Type;`

5. (i) `mysql>SELECT CURDATE();`

   Output `2021-11-01`

   (ii) `mysql>SELECT INSTR("CORPORATE LAWYER", ''OR");`

   Output `2`

   (iii) `SELECT * FROM Students ORDER BY AGGREGATE, NAME DESC;`

Or (i) 64

   (ii) 88

   (iii) `SELECT Name, Class FROM Students WHERE Course_name IS NULL OR Course_Name LIKE "%economics";`

6. (i) DAYNAME(DATE(curdate()))

   (ii) LTRIM(" Python")

   (iii) MONTHNAME(date(dob))

   (iv) INSTR("Information Technology","Information")

   (v) POW(a,b)

7. (i) (a) Satellite communication

(b) Bluetooth or infrared whichever is supported by the phone.

(ii) Domain in http://www.cbsenic.in/aboutus.htm is "www.cbsenic.in".

Or (i) HyperText Transfer Protocol

(ii) Advanced Research Projects Agency NETwork

(iii) Virtual Private Network

(iv) Modulator Demodulator

(v) Transmission Control Protocol/Internet Protocol

(vi) Domain Name System

8. The call quality of cloud communciations systems depends on the speed and reliability of your Internet. You will hear a vast improvement in call quality compared to traditional landlines. Landlines don't have as much audio bandwidth, which can result in muffled or fuzzy calls.

VoIP calles achieve this through HD voice technology.

Find out your Internet speed by taking the VoIP speed test.

Or (i) Most suitable layout according to distance is

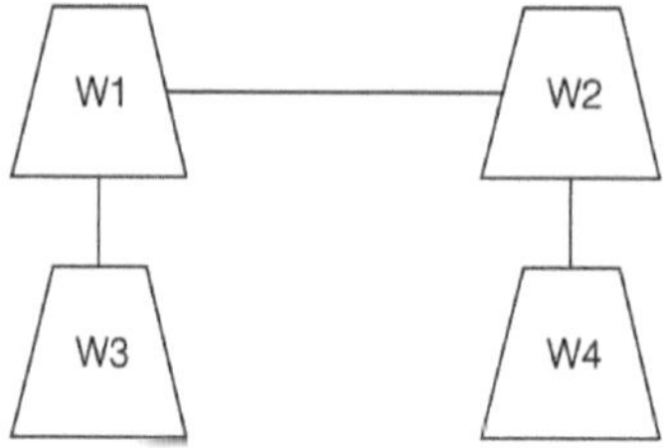

(ii) Star topology

(iii) Broadband

(iv) (a) Repeaters may be skipped as per above layout   (because distance is less than 100 m).

(b) In every wing

(v) Radiowaves

9. (i) Primary Key – Rollno

(ii) Degree of table= 5

(iii) `INSERT INTO Fees VALUES(101,'Aman','XII',5000);`

(iv) `DELETE FROM Fees;`

(v) `Describe Fees;`

Or (i) `SELECT Name FROM Sports WHERE Grade1='A' OR Grade2='A';`

(ii) `SELECT COUNT(*) FROM Sports Where Game1='Cricket' OR Game2='Cricket';`

(iii) `SELECT Name FROM Sports WHERE Game1=Game2;`

(iv) `SELECT Game1,Game2 FROM Sports WHERE Name LIKE 'A%';`

(v) 6

(vi) 7

8

9

10

(vii) 10

(viii) 2

2

1

1

Printed by Libri Plureos GmbH in Hamburg,
Germany